MW01048103

Can the battle for LIFE in the womb still be won in America? Yes! As a lifelong defender of LIFE in the womb, and as an OB/GYN for over 25 years, I have gained new understanding, wisdom, and tools on how this battle can, and must be won. Roland does not just share his feelings and thoughts; he shares true data from large scale national surveys, interviews, and doctrinally sound biblical principles that everyone can apply to successfully defend the Image of God in the womb. Roland blends stories of Adam and Eve; Joseph and the Angel, personal experiences, Biblical principles and the Gospel perfectly. **This treatise is an excellent guide on how we can have victory and experience national Pro Abundant Life!** A must read for the Church!

Dr. William Lile, *D.O., FACOG, Founder ProLifeDoc.org*

In his book "The Alternative to Abortion: Why We Must Be Pro Abundant Life" Roland Warren kindly and carefully lays out a case for not only the value of life, but the call of Jesus Christ to a purposeful and fulfilling life for all. In an engaging and common sense way, **Roland helps us view this topic through a unique, fresh lens. His perspective is not only refreshing, it is extremely instructional, and truly inspiring.** He is an astute thinker, and a clear and very effective communicator. It's a book worthy of your time!

Dale O'Shields, *Senior Pastor, Church of the Redeemer, Gaithersburg, MD*

As the limits of political solutions to the abortion crisis become clear, Roland Warren's book provides the alternative that pro-life Americans, especially Christians, have been searching for. As a pastor whose purpose is to make disciples for Jesus Christ, **I am confident that this book is the breath of fresh air that the pro-life movement needs to direct much-needed attention to the Church as the way to finally win our battle against abortion.**

Rev. Samuel Rodriguez, *Lead Pastor, New Season Church, President, National Hispanic Christian Leadership Conference.*

My good friend Roland Warren has given us a powerful tool for both understanding and implementing a pro abundant life agenda that not only seeks to protect the physical life of the unborn but also the spiritual life, restoration, and development for mother, father and child. **This book is a must-read for those who want to obey Christ in fulfilling the Great Commandment and Great Commission for the strengthening of the family and equipping the church in addressing those facing the challenge of an unplanned pregnancy.**

Dr. Tony Evans, *President, The Urban Alternative*

This is a critical moment in the defense of innocent pre-born lives. What lies ahead is the hard, long-term work to shape hearts and minds, to influence our neighbors at the worldview level. **Roland Warren provides a game plan here, one that holds together truth and love, clear on not only what we must oppose but what we must champion.** It's time to roll up our sleeves and get to work.

John Stonestreet, *President of the Colson Center and Host of BreakPoint*

This extraordinary book is about so much more than a particular decision made at a point in time. **Warren's call to be pro *abundant* life restarts and resets the conversation about abortion. It is not primarily a political concern. It is a discipleship call that encompasses life, marriage, family, cultural assumptions, social commitments, and the very mission of the church.** Rooted in Scripture and richly illustrated with stories to make sense of the statistics, this book is an essential resource for situating the specific issue of abortion within the expansive context of the abundant life that Jesus offers the church and the world.

Walter Kim, *President of the National Association of Evangelicals*

In this book **Roland Warren presents a plan that is engaging, refreshing and compelling based on facts, life experience and most importantly, scripture.** I pray this book will be read by thousands of pro-life and pro-choice proponents motivating us to work as never before for a culture of life.

Sylvia Slifko, *ICU Mobile founder*

Roland brings needed clarity and new insights to a complex issue. His complete understanding of why men and women choose abortion will stir you to pray and act differently. Because Roland understands the problems that lead to abortion decisions, his solutions and recommendations will work. His use of Scripture, careful use of vocabulary, and challenge to us to do the same make this a strong book. Read it and follow through. Buy one for your pastor and Christian school administrators. Roland includes realistic ideas we can all implement. We must take this book seriously!

Kathy Koch, *PhD, Founder, Celebrate Kids, Inc., and the author of Five to Thrive & Resilient Kids*

THE
ALTERNATIVE
TO
ABORTION

THE

ALTERNATIVE

TO

ABORTION

WHY WE MUST BE
PRO ABUNDANT LIFE

ROLAND C. WARREN

Cover and Interior Design: Rachel Parker
Editor: Susan Hobbs

PUBLISHED BY: Care Net

Library of Congress Control Number: 2024916483

The Alternative to Abortion: Why We Must Be Pro Abundant Life/ Roland C. Warren

ISBN: 978-0-9972285-3-3 (hardcover), 978-0-9972285-4-0 (paperback), 978-0-9972285-6-4 (e-book)

To Yvette, my beloved
and my hero...

TABLE OF
CONTENTS

FOREWORD

BY DAVID PLATT

Certain biblical truths are incontrovertible when it comes to the issue of abortion, and to deny them is to disregard God himself. While I don't presume this list is exhaustive, I will mention eight of these truths here.

1. **A mother's womb holds a person who is known, loved, and formed by God.** According to Psalm 139, God's fearful and wonderful creating work begins at conception, and the miracle of human formation that follows is a testimony to the glory of our Divine Designer.

2. **Every single person bears the image of God and possesses value before God.** This is true of every single child inside and outside a womb, every single man and woman, and every single person with any special need.

3. **Every single person deserves honor from us**. In a world where so much pro-choice rhetoric revolves around honoring women in ways that dishonor (and eventually discard) a child in their womb and so much pro-life rhetoric revolves around honoring a child in a womb while dishonoring various challenges women face, God's Word says all people are worthy of honor, including both a child and a woman who carries that child. God is their champion, and we should be the same.

4. **God ordains marriage for the making and rearing of children, and God designs sexual activity exclusively for marriage between a man and a woman**. In my country, approximately 87% of women seeking abortions are unmarried. Addressing abortion necessarily involves understanding a biblical view of singleness, marriage, and sexuality.

5. **God gives government for the good of people and the legislation of morality.** God entrusts governments with the responsibility of protecting all people, including children, women, and men, and it is right for government to create and implement laws designed for all of their protection.

6. **God requires his people to do justice and love kindness for all people.** Followers of Jesus have a responsibility to do justice for children in the womb and out of the womb, as well as for the women and men who are their parents. In my country, approximately 75% of women seeking abortions are living near or below the poverty line, and in one recent survey of 1000 women who had abortions, over 75% of them said they would have preferred to parent had their circumstances been different. These statistics shout for God's people to do justice in myriad ways beyond merely voting in an election.

7. **God calls his people to believe and speak unpopular truth as we show and express unexpected love.** All of these biblical affirmations concerning abortion go against the cultural grain, but God's people do not have the option of compromising on his Word. Yet even as God's Word is on our lips, his love must be evident in our lives. The church should be the most kind, compassionate, tender, and sacrificially loving people for moms and dads in pregnancy, for women who have had abortions, and for people and politicians who disagree with what the Bible teaches.

8. **Jesus commands his church to accomplish a great commission, not to win political elections.** To be clear, we work for just laws and leaders and policies and practices. However, our ultimate aim is not new laws, but new hearts, and only the gospel of Jesus Christ can do this work.

The aim of followers of Jesus is not merely for abortion to be illegal in government, but for abortion to be unthinkable in people's hearts and minds, and only God by His grace and the work of His Spirit can bring that about through disciples of Jesus making disciples of Jesus in and through the church.

I met Roland Warren not too long after moving to pastor in metro Washington, D.C., and I am so glad I did. Since that time, he has become a good friend. I laugh when I think back to my first meeting with him. He had so much to share and what he was sharing was so good that by the end of our time, I had pages of notes I had written down. Ever since then, in every conversation with Roland, I inevitably take notes. That's one reason I'm thankful he's written this book—so that I can have what he's saying in front of me instead of having to write it all down!

In all seriousness, the book you hold in your hand is a treasure trove of truth from the heart and mind of a man who loves God and loves people and I believe is leading the way on the issue of abortion in the church and in my country. Roland is a sharp, wise thinker—a graduate of Princeton and the Wharton School of Business at Penn. But far more important than his intellectual gifts, he is a faithful husband and dad who faced an unexpected pregnancy before he was married and made a decision to not just raise that child, but to work for other children, moms, and dads like them. He has done this work for decades now, and he has helped me see the unmistakable links between the gospel, the great commission, the church, abortion, and the world in ways that I long for others to see. The more people read this book, from everyday men and women to pastors and politicians, the more we will be able to faithfully do justice amidst the modern holocaust of abortion in our day.

I wholeheartedly commend this book to you, and I pray that God will bless it so that multitudes of children (inside and outside of the womb), women, and men made in his image might experience the abundant life we have been fearfully and wonderfully made to live.

ACKNOWLEDGMENT

First, I want to thank God for his guidance and care. The pro abundant life perspective detailed in this book is a result of the wisdom and insight God has given me. If we let him, He will take the ashes of our sins and failings and use them for His glory and the benefit of others. Amen!

Second, I want to thank my amazing and Godly wife Yvette for her steadfast courage so many years ago. My pro abundant life journey started with her.

Third, anyone who has written a book knows that even though their name is on the cover, the book would not be possible without the help of so many others. In my case, I am so thankful to Heather Creekmore who helped me get the pro abundant life perspective out of my head and onto paper. Vince DiCaro has also been instrumental over the years in helping me discuss and work through the pro abundant life approach. And I'm especially thankful to Rachel Parker for her amazing creative and graphic skills that made this book so compelling and visually engaging. Many thanks also to Susan Hobbs for her fantastic editing work.

Finally, I want to especially thank Care Net's board and so many others who have strongly encouraged me to write this book. God really used them to inspire me to get this book done.

CHAPTER ONE

WHY I CHOSE LIFE

"What's a nice girl like you doing out on a night like this?"

"Really corny!" she replied. A slow smile spread across her face, and I knew the line was more effective than she would admit. I walked her back to her dorm. It was clear from the start we had a special connection.

Yvette was a cute freshman, just one year behind me at Princeton. We lived in the same dorm and shared the same cafeteria, where I'd see her now and then. I thought she was cute and wanted to meet her, but I was shy. So when the opportunity to regale her with a corny pickup line presented itself after football practice one day, I took my shot. I had no idea how that brief conversation was about to change everything.

Yvette and I were soon inseparable. We ate our meals together, spent all our time together, and fell in love. We were both Christians. We knew what we were supposed to do. But we found ourselves in love at college with not a lot of supervision. Eventually, we became intimate.

I knew well what the risks were with this kind of behavior, but let's just say they weren't front of mind. Until one day, while I was home on a midterm break, I got a call from Yvette.

"I think I'm pregnant," she whispered nervously.

These are the only words I remember her saying, because after that everything went into slow motion. This was a life-defining moment. I didn't have a framework for what would happen next. I wouldn't say I panicked, but the weight of an uncertain future felt heavier than ever.

You're Going to Have an Abortion, Aren't You?

We returned from the break and Yvette went to the clinic on campus to confirm what she already knew to be true. The first thing the nurse asked her, or (more accurately) told her was, "You're going to have an abortion, aren't you?" Yvette said no. She explained to the nurse that she wanted to get married, have her baby, and raise her child.

Undeterred, the nurse continued her interrogation. "What year are you?"

"A sophomore."

"Well, what do you want to do when you graduate?"

"I want to become a doctor."

"Well, how are you going to get through Princeton, let alone medical school, with a baby? How will you ever be a doctor with a baby?"

Yvette didn't know. Would all her dreams end here? *What if the nurse was right?* It seemed far easier to focus on what would be lost if we had this baby versus what could be gained. Plus, we were told that Princeton would pay for the abortion but not the delivery. So, as near-penniless college students, we were on our own.

Back in the dorm room, we sat on the edge of the bed (which is obviously where we should have spent all our time), and talked it all through. Yvette was shell-shocked at the lack of support she received. The nurse was an older woman—maybe even a mother herself. She could have said, "Ok, let's see how we can make your 'choice' work. Would you consider placing the baby for adoption? Let me help you." Or, she could have asked, "Who's the father? Can he come to your next visit? Let's make sure that he is prepared to support your choice and his child." But she didn't. Instead, the nurse suggested an abortion and cast a negative light on Yvette's life should she decide to give birth.

So, there we were—on the edge of the bed. We didn't want to compli-cate one mistake with a second mistake. We were Christians and knew God's standard and what he required. At the same time, we were in a community of Christians. We knew this would certainly be embarrassing. Covering it up with abortion may have helped us "save face" in church on Sunday mornings, but we were determined not to focus on that.

We wanted to get married and had already talked about our future to-gether. No, it wasn't our plan to have a baby first and then get married. Yet we knew God was there. He was, somehow, in the middle of all of it. He hadn't left us or forsaken us, even in our mistakes. He would be with us through the hard journey ahead.

We had only just begun to understand how hard it would be. Each of us had to tell our parents. Yvette was so scared to tell her father. She had been hiding the pregnancy for four months from folks on campus, but she was beginning to show. I urged her to write him a letter. A week or so passed, and then she got the call from him. He said, "I love you, and if you want to get married, you can get married. If you don't want to get married, you can come home."

He was also clear that if we did get married, we were going to have to be adults. We would be on our own.

The first person I told about the pregnancy was my mother. I can still hear the disappointment in her voice. I was the first person to have a shot at graduating from college, and attending Princeton was a very big deal. She was understandably concerned that an unplanned pregnancy would stop me from graduating.

My path to Princeton had not been particularly easy. My parents split up when I was about seven, so I grew up without my dad. My mom had my older brother at age seventeen and me at nineteen. My two younger siblings were born shortly after that. At age twenty-three, my mom was a single mother with four kids under eight years of age. To go from that situation to a place like Princeton was pretty unique. My mom was proud of me, and had hopes and dreams related to what I would do with my Ivy League education. She was worried that if we had this baby she would see her life story revisited in me. But I was committed to a different vision. I knew I didn't want to repeat the pattern I'd grown up with.

As a kid, I loved watching *The Brady Bunch*. I remember comparing that family to my own experience and seeing no similarities. Many of my aunts and cousins were single mothers, and my community seemed to be what I call a single-mother culture where there weren't a lot of married men around. Seeing men who were husbands and fathers on TV shows or at church was aspirational for me. On some level, I recognized that something in my life was missing, and I didn't want to repeat that same cycle in any way, shape, or form.

In any case, soon after telling our parents, we stood before the justice of the peace in Princeton, New Jersey, surrounded by a few college friends, and we said our "I do's." Yvette was five months pregnant, beaming with radiant joy. Because they didn't offer transitional housing at school, Yvette went home to Texas to have the baby. I stayed on campus, worked, and began to play football for another season.

In late August, while the team was in two-a-day training sessions, I got a call that it was time for our baby to arrive. I traveled to Texas for our scheduled delivery. We had a beautiful, seven-pound, fifteen-ounce boy.

That was the beginning of our life as a family. Unplanned, absolutely. But, by God's grace, He turned our hearts back to Him. We decided to choose life for our son, and plan for our future together as husband and wife. So, although we had an unplanned pregnancy, we didn't have a crisis pregnancy because we created a family.

Choosing a Life Together

So, by God's grace, this part of my story has a very happy ending. It seems that nurse who told Yvette that she'd never graduate from Princeton with a baby was right. Yvette didn't graduate with just one baby, she graduated with two.

Yvette came back to school in her junior year. Toward the beginning of her senior year, we got pregnant again with our second son, Justin. Yvette delivered Justin just a few weeks before her senior thesis was due. Within two weeks she had two big due dates and met them both! There's an amazing picture of

Yvette carrying Justin at her graduation. A photographer was there, and he captured the shot of her with our little guy strapped on through the whole ceremony. That's not something you see at Princeton graduations very often.

When someone suggests an abortion, it's often based on the premise that nothing good can come from the birth of the child. The child is a net negative for the mother, the family, and society at large. But the nurse was wrong about Yvette's future career. She did go on to become a medical doctor. In fact, she was the chief resident of her program (though she's far too humble to ever tell you that). She's been practicing medicine for more than thirty years now.

I am reminded of the adage that anyone can tell you how many seeds are in an apple, but only God can tell you how many apples are in a single seed. That's why it's so dangerous for us to try and control life by deciding who should and should not live based on our limited perception. The baby they wanted us to throw in a trash can, our firstborn son, went on to graduate from Harvard. Also, we have a beautiful granddaughter, a blessing we would have missed if Yvette had followed the nurse's advice.

 Unexpectedly, the narrative of my story became tied to my fatherhood story. I earned a master of business administration degree from the University of Pennsylvania's Wharton School of Business and worked for large corporations including IBM, PepsiCo, and Goldman Sachs. However, I could never shake the nudge that God had work for me to do that would directly connect to the decision Yvette and I made to have the baby, and the decision I made to be a husband and a father.

About twenty years after our first son was born, I had the opportunity to lead the National Fatherhood Initiative and work in innovative ways to inspire other men to be the best dads they can be. At the same time, God graciously gave me the perfect space to work through my own issues related to being raised without my dad.

In 2012, I came to Care Net, a national Christian ministry that offers compassion, hope, and help to women and men at risk for abortion, ready to learn, grow, and ask questions. As I look back on my life, I can see how God connected the dots and led me to this place and this work. My passion for the life issue stems from my own story and observations of the challenges addressing this difficult issue. Consequently, with God's leading, I've developed a somewhat novel approach to addressing the abortion issue. I believe this approach, through the power of God's Holy Spirit, has tremendous power to transform hearts and lives on the issue of abortion.

That said, I know exactly what it's like to be confronted with that moment—that moment when you must choose life and the choice feels daunting, heavy, and uncertain. It's easy to say what you'd do when confronted with that decision. But a whole different paradigm exists when you're the one in the position to make it. I knew the so-called easier way out. Yet, deciding to be a husband to Yvette and a father to our children was the best decision I could have ever made. I thank God that He gave me the grace and perspective to do that as a twenty-year-old. Now, I hope to encourage others who face the same difficult decision to follow a similar path.

I also hope to encourage you. Even if you're far beyond the childbearing years, even if making your own "life decision" is something you've never faced or never will face, you need to know what an important role you play in helping others choose life.

Our life stories are never wasted, because God is the perfect author. Who could have ever guessed that the guy who got his girlfriend pregnant in college would someday, forty years later, be working to help other women and men choose life? As they say, "God doesn't call the equipped, He equips the called."

1. We got married in Princeton by a justice of the peace with a few student friends present. This is our only wedding picture. I don't know where I am looking...

2. Yvette at 19 years old – Godly, Smart, Beautiful, and Courageous!

3. After our wedding, I carried Yvette over the threshold of our new home...her dorm room.

4. Yvette in the procession to get her diploma at her Princeton graduation ceremony. A photographer saw her and took this picture. We were not trying to "go viral" or make news. Our second son, Justin, needed to eat so she strapped him on!

Starting school early

Justin Lopez-Warren, 2-months old, might not recall his first day at school, but his mom, Yvette, 23, certainly will. She carried him to her graduation ceremony at Princeton yesterday.

5. I love this picture. It's from one of our first official dates.

6. Well, the nurse who encouraged Yvette to have an abortion was right about one thing. Yvette didn't graduate from Princeton with a baby. She graduated with two. Justin was born about a month or so before she graduated. She is truly an amazing woman!

7. Yvette graduating from medical school. An amazing accomplishment. Nothing is impossible with God.

8. We renewed our wedding vows on our tenth anniversary. I loved seeing Yvette in a wedding dress. Beautiful.

9. Yvette in her medical residency during her obstetrics rotation delivering her first baby. She has been a family practice doctor for nearly thirty years.

10.

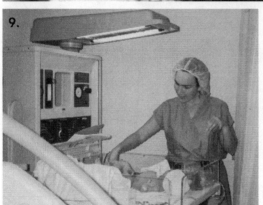

WALSON AIR FORCE
MEDICAL FACILITY

Name: Dr. Lopez-Warren

Duty Section: Family Practice

305th Medical Group (NM) Form 99   Feb 95

10. After her medical residency, Yvette joined the Air Force and rose to the rank of Major. She was even selected as medical provider of the year for the entire base!

11. Forty-two years of marriage and counting. God is good!

CHAPTER TWO

WHY PRO ABUNDANT LIFE?

*The thief comes only to steal and kill and destroy. I came that they
may have life and have it abundantly.*

John 10:10

During my first year at Care Net, I spent a lot of time asking questions. I
visited our affiliated pregnancy centers, scoured the data we'd collected from
decades of serving women and men facing pregnancy decisions. I also searched
scripture, prayed, and asked God to show me how to see issues of life through
the lens of His word. One day, while reading the New Testament, I realized
this shocking truth: Jesus wasn't pro-life.

Wait!

Before you throw this book across the room in frustration, please allow
me to explain. In John 10:10, Christ said He came not just to give us life but
abundant life. In Greek, there are two primary words for life: *bios* and *zoe*. *Bios*
refers to our physical life. This is the root of the word *biology*. When Christ
talks about the "cares and riches and pleasures of life" (Luke 8:14), He uses
the word *bios*. *Zoe* refers to a unique spiritual life, the divine life uniquely
possessed by God.

When Christ says, "I have come that they may have life and may have it abundantly," He is speaking in terms of both *bios* and *zoe*.

This is why I don't believe Jesus was pro-life. Or maybe a better way to say it is that Jesus wasn't just pro-life. He was pro *abundant* life. You see, if Jesus walked the earth today, His mission would go further than just saving babies from abortion. His goal was not just life for the here and now, but life for all eternity. Christ came to give *zoe* life to all—both inside and outside the womb.

When you think about it, John 10:10 is truly Jesus's "why" statement. Why did Jesus come? For the purpose of abundant life. *Bios* life is important too, no doubt. It is good when babies are spared from the atrocities of abortion, but scripture teaches us that's not enough. Jesus doesn't stop there. After all, an atheist can be pro-life—focused on just saving the *bios* life. But Jesus is about the *zoe* life too. In other words, it's not just about heartbeats, but about heartbeats that are heaven bound.

At Care Net, we coined the term "pro abundant life" to describe our unique approach to the life issue. In fact, we're so passionate about this approach that if you ask any of the members of our staff if Care Net is a pro-life ministry, they may say no. Hopefully, they'll quickly follow up by explaining that Care Net is a pro abundant life ministry.

Please understand. We're not trying to be clever, pithy, difficult, or challenging. This isn't a marketing ploy or corporate rebranding. There's an important biblical reason for our language here. If this was Jesus's why statement, then shouldn't this also be ours?

When you look closely at John 10:10 in Greek, the word "abundantly" comes from *perisson,* which means superabundant in terms of quantity. It literally means to exceed a number, need, or measure. This is not like asking a fast-food restaurant to supersize a drink order. This is about superabundance. This is taking the cup that you already have to the fountain and watching it overflow. Abundant life means a life that's overflowing.

Perisson also means superior in terms of quality, such as in a relationship. The highest quality relationship anyone can have is with God. Adam and Eve had *perisson* in the garden of Eden. They had an intimacy with God that no one else experienced because they lived without sin in the presence of righteousness.

Now, because of their sin (and our own), we've been separated from that high-quality, superabundant relationship with God. At least we were, until Jesus. And that's what Jesus is saying in John 10:10. He's telling us that He came to take us all the way back to the garden of Eden. As author Gary Moon reminds us, we are all homesick for Eden.[1] But Jesus, the creator and sustainer of Eden, is the only way back. As the second Adam, He'll take us back to the garden and restore what Adam messed up. The kind of life Jesus advocated for was the abundant life where we live in close relationship with Him in terms of both quality and quantity. Jesus sacrificed his *bios* on the cross so that we could have *zoe* life with him for eternity.

Expanding the Vision

For fifty years the pro-life movement has done good work fighting for *bios* both politically and materially. If you ask someone on the street if they're pro-life, they'll probably prove it by telling you who they voted for or which organization they're financially supporting that provides material support for women at risk for abortion. There's certainly an important role and need for both political engagement and material support within the movement. But from a Christian perspective, the life issue is not primarily about political engagement or material support. It's about something greater.

Those who are pro abundant life have a responsibility to engage politically and materially as a byproduct of following Christ and His commandments. But the pro abundant life call of Christ must reach beyond just saving babies for *bios* life on this planet. If a woman comes to a pregnancy center and decides to have her second or third baby with no husband or committed father anywhere in sight, that is a pro-life win because a life was saved. But as Christians we should not be comfortable declaring victory simply when a baby is born rather than aborted. It seems shortsighted to count it a win for a woman to deliver a baby and then immediately become a single mother dependent on social services support. It's transactional. Yes, we've saved a life. But based on statistics, that child is at risk for some of the most intractable social ills such as poverty, low academic performance, incarceration, and even abortion. The child's mother is at risk for another unplanned pregnancy and potential abortion as well. Without a vision for and model of God's design for the family, the pro-life movement lacks the power to break the cycle.

Jesus's call is to come as you are but not to stay as you came. Instead, "be transformed by the renewal of your mind" (Romans 12:2). When a woman comes back to a pregnancy center with a new baby from a different man, she is not transformed. The gospel transforms us. Jesus didn't come just so we could have life, but so we could have abundant life. If we save babies without transforming lives, we're missing the mission Jesus set before us.

Discovering the "abundant life" angle was a critical part of my journey. I've gotten some pushback over the years that this "distracts" pro-lifers from their mission, but I disagree. As I hope you'll soon understand, there's no more effective way for us to transform hearts and minds on the issue of abortion than to make Jesus's call for us to help others have abundant life central to our mission and work.

Care Net's pro abundant life vision can be viewed as a structure with two main pillars: God's design for family and God's call to discipleship.

The first pillar is family. In the very first chapter of the New Testament, Matthew begins with a family genealogy connecting familiar names like Abraham and David from the Old Testament all the way to Joseph, Mary's husband and Jesus's earthly father. Immediately after this list of fathers and families, we find the story of Jesus's birth (Matthew 1:18–25). The most famous story in the whole Bible—the story of Jesus's birth—models what is to be done when a woman faces a pregnancy decision and shows God's heart for the sanctity of life, marriage, and family. Beyond scripture, data supports that abortion is least likely to happen in a situation where mom and dad are married.[2] The safest place for a baby to find *bios* life is in the biblical construct of marriage and family.

The second pillar of the pro abundant life framework is discipleship. Specifically, this means seeing women and men at risk for abortion as those who need to become disciples of Jesus Christ. The model for this also comes from the book of Matthew. At Care Net, we envision a culture where women and men faced with pregnancy decisions are transformed by the gospel of Jesus Christ and empowered to choose life for their unborn children and abundant life for their families.

We prefer the term pregnancy decisions as opposed to unplanned pregnancies because only a woman has an unplanned pregnancy, but everyone involved has a pregnancy decision. When a woman becomes pregnant, she is not the only one facing the pregnancy decision. The father has a pregnancy decision and their community has a pregnancy decision. But before we examine what scripture and data show to be the best way to prevent abortion, let's take a look at why women choose to have abortions. It's probably not what you would expect.

PART ONE:

GOD'S DESIGN FOR THE FAMILY

CHAPTER THREE

WHY DO WOMEN WANT ABORTIONS?

A few years ago, I spoke at a fundraising dinner for a Care Net affiliated pregnancy center. We enjoyed a great meal, heard inspirational messages, and felt those warm, fuzzy feelings about the important work we're doing in saving the lives of babies. The crowd was energized.

Afterward, a man came up to me, ready to affirm his support for our cause. "I just can't imagine why a woman would even have an abortion. I can't get my head around that," he declared. There was a hint of judgment in his tone, but I tried to understand where he was coming from. It's easy to believe you'd always decide for life when you're living a comfortable life with enough resources, emotional support, stability, and security. I, too, once had difficulty understanding why someone would decide to end a baby's life.

Advances in medical technology make it even more difficult to understand how someone would make that choice. Science now easily proves what the Bible teaches: at conception, a unique individual comes into existence. Hair and eye color, and to some extent, personality and intelligence, are established at conception. A baby's heart beats just twenty-two days after fertilization. The modern window into the womb, ultrasound, allows us to see more clearly than ever the life growing inside of a pregnant woman.

Yet even the acknowledgment that the unborn baby is a life, the recognition that this God-created child is a living human being, isn't enough to stop people from making an abortion decision. Let me take that one step further. This knowledge isn't even enough to stop many Christians, people sitting in our pews on Sundays, from making abortion decisions.

Did you know this?

Pro-life advocacy groups have done an effective job at spreading their message. To some degree, they could declare "mission accomplished!" because most in our culture believe that a fetus in the womb is a life. But what if that doesn't even matter anymore? What if the main reason why women have abortions doesn't have anything to do with whether or not they believe that baby is a life?

Every good marketer strives to find the "why" behind each consumer decision. We would be wise to follow that line of thought when it comes to abortion decisions. I believe there are two main categories of women who choose abortion: those without support and those who have adopted the concept of the modern self.

The Chart That Shaped How I See the Abortion Issue

Early in my tenure at Care Net, God gave me an insight that truly helped me understand a key reason why women have abortions. As a business guy, I'm a big fan of charts, so I created one entitled, "Support Needed by Mothers and Children." On the y-axis, I listed the type of support needed: physical, emotional, social, and spiritual. On the x-axis, I listed the time this support is needed, starting with conception to birth and ongoing. Then, I drew a line from conception upward to the right reflecting that the support needed by mothers and children increases over time. The area below this line represented the support women facing pregnancy decisions needed.

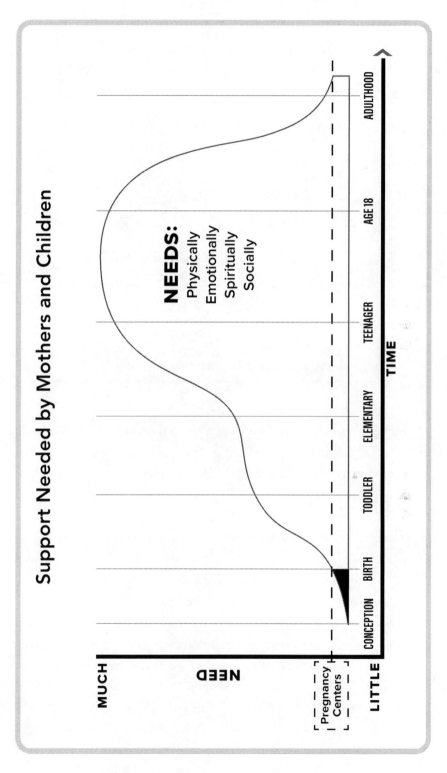

Support Needed by Mothers and Children

NEEDS:
Physically
Emotionally
Spiritually
Socially

MUCH

NEED

LITTLE

Pregnancy
Centers

CONCEPTION BIRTH TODDLER ELEMENTARY TEENAGER AGE 18 ADULTHOOD

TIME

Looking at this chart, I had an epiphany that helped me see why some women were at risk for abortion more than others. I shaded the area between conception and birth as the sweet spot of support that pregnancy centers provide.

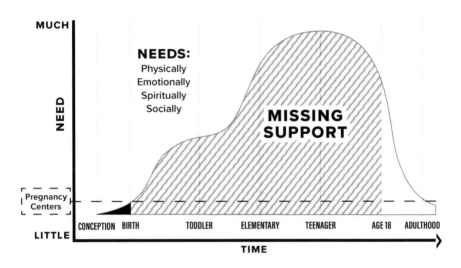

Support Needed by Mothers and Children

But there was a big problem—the missing support from birth onward that pregnancy centers could not provide. This was the abortion dilemma that every woman dealing with an unplanned pregnancy faced. No matter how caring and compassionate a pregnancy center may be, too often a woman makes her decision about abortion based on the support she has or does not have from birth onward. So, for many women, this issue is about *nine months and one second.*

My wife faced this dilemma because this missing support area represented her hopes, dreams, and aspirations for her life. Her nurse focused only on this missing support when she strongly recommended abortion. And this is the problem area for every woman at an abortion clinic or at a pregnancy center. To the degree that a woman cannot see how she can fill the missing support, she is much more likely to have an abortion.

I realized Care Net's ministry model had to address the missing support challenge for women at risk for abortion. Now, God is wise. He has a design to cover the missing support—husbands and fathers. The sanctity of marriage and family as God designed is very much linked to the sanctity of life. Consequently, it's not surprising that the data says that 87 percent of women who have abortions are unmarried.[1]

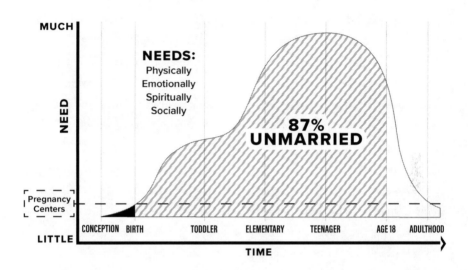

Support Needed by Mothers and Children

My wife was less likely to be at risk for abortion because she had someone who said he would be a husband to her and a father to the child growing inside of her. For many women who choose abortion, missing support is their primary challenge. Either they fear they don't have support now, or they fear they won't have support in the future.

Peter's Denial of Jesus

Let's go back to the concerns of my friend from the pregnancy center dinner. In his paradigm, it doesn't make any sense that a woman who understands what is right wouldn't make the "right" decision. This is hard for most of us to wrap our heads around. To help him better understand what happens when a woman decides to have an abortion, I shared this story from scripture.

Peter was one of Jesus's earliest and most committed followers. In fact, he was part of a select inner circle, along with James and John, who experienced things the other disciples didn't. Peter displayed moments of remarkable faith, such as when he left the safety of a boat in the midst of a storm to walk on water to reach Jesus. Most importantly, he answered rightly when Jesus asked Peter who he believed He was. Without hesitation, Peter responded, "You are the Messiah, the Son of the living God" (Matthew 16:16 NIV). After this, Jesus bestowed the highest compliment on Peter. He promised to build his church on the kind of rock-solid faith that Peter demonstrated.

Despite all this, in Matthew 26:69–75, after Jesus had been arrested, Peter sat around a fire warming himself as Jesus was being interrogated. He had followed Jesus from a distance because he did not want to be exposed. A servant girl noticed him and accused him of being one of Jesus's followers. Peter firmly denied it.

Then, when Peter was heading out of the city gateway, another servant girl saw him and suggested that he was with Jesus. Peter denied it, again. Finally, a little while later, a group approached Peter. They, too, attested that surely he was a follower of Jesus. For a third time, Peter denied it, this time with a curse just to make it clear that he was angry at the mere suggestion of it.

Then, when that rooster crowed, Jesus looked straight at Peter. Their eyes locked. And Peter was instantly reminded of Jesus's words, "Before the rooster crows, you will disown me three times."

Peter fled in despair. Can you imagine how sick to his stomach he must have felt? Peter had "aborted" Jesus.

You see, abortion isn't just about the physical act of killing an unborn baby. It's also the rejection of one life in the favor of another—the decision that one life is worth more than another life. Abortion reflects a worldview as old as sin.

I've always considered the first sin to be the first "abortion." Eve, with a silent Adam complicit at her side, essentially declared, "My Body, My Choice!" as she tasted the forbidden fruit and shared it with her husband. With the juice still moist on their lips, they declared in unison to the creator of life, "I know what is better for my life and for my future than you do!"

Despite their intimacy with God, Eve and Adam rejected their relationship with Him.

Peter did the same.

As he sat by the fire, Peter knew who Jesus was. He knew Jesus was not just a life, but also the Way, the Truth, *and* the Life. But at that moment, Jesus was a life worth sacrificing. Jesus was a life worth denying. Jesus was the answer he didn't want to choose. Why?

Because Peter was afraid.

Think about Peter's circumstances. How could he not have been afraid? Peter knew well that Jesus faced persecution and likely death, life-altering events. If Peter were exposed as a Jesus follower, Peter's life would be changed too. Peter likely still held a deeply embedded notion that Jesus would be a warrior king, not a suffering king. As a key follower of Jesus, Peter may have desired to share in Jesus's temporal victory. Peter had hopes and dreams for his life with Jesus. But, when stressed, pressed, and under duress, Peter was not willing to risk his own life by acknowledging Jesus's life.

Peter was also alone.

Just imagine if Peter, a man who had demonstrated considerable courage, had been sitting by that fire with his eleven brothers in Christ. Earlier that same evening, surrounded by friends, Peter had the daring determination to draw his sword to protect Jesus when he was being arrested. But hours later, all by himself, Peter wouldn't even risk defending Jesus with a mere mumble of, "Yes, I know him."

Proverbs 11:14 declares that "in an abundance of counselors there is safety." And there is courage, too. When we are isolated and alone, especially when we're afraid, it's much easier to deny what we know to be true. That applies to Peter. That applies to the woman facing an abortion decision. That applies to all of us.

I've spoken to countless women and men who have aborted their babies. Not surprisingly, when they recount their stories, they have much in common with Peter's dilemma. Despite echoes of pro-choice messaging that declares life in the womb is just a "glob of cells," these men and women didn't believe this when they had their abortions. They knew the baby was a life, but the baby was a life worth sacrificing because the circumstances of their pregnancy made it so.

Too often, women are alone when they make their abortion decisions. Due to the increased availability of the abortion pill, they are also alone when they have their abortion. Sadly, the pro-choice rhetoric, "My Body, My Choice" worked. Women facing unplanned pregnancies retreat into isolation to determine what to do while men, much like the first man, Adam, remain silent because they've been brainwashed into believing that because legally it is "her choice," they hold no moral responsibility.

In Peter's story we can find hope as we lovingly reach out to those who face life decisions. God is a God of reason, so of course it is important to appeal to an expecting parent's sense of reason. The fact that the baby is alive is important, but misses the opportunity to acknowledge and validate the mother's concerns and needs. As ministers of reconciliation and restoration, we must gently remind her that the covenant relationship between parents and a baby is a blessing from above. We must show her how God can be a part of her story. And we must approach her with great compassion and understanding for how scared and alone she must feel. Because like Peter, we too were once deniers of the Way, the Truth, and the Life…until we weren't.

Isolated and Alone

We must be able to see ourselves in a woman's story if we are going to help her. Then we can connect. Peter was missing support and made an unthinkable decision. This is what happens in the case of most women who choose abortion. Can't we all relate to a time in our lives when we weren't courageous because we were isolated and alone? Everyone knows how it feels to be excluded and facing rejection. Once we can see abortion decisions through this lens, we can meet people at their point of need. We can empathize. We can relate. And that's how we minister to them most effectively. It's not through eyes of judgment but through compassion and the grace of Jesus.

If we continue to only ask questions like, "How could you kill your child?" we miss out on a tremendous opportunity to minister to those facing pregnancy decisions. Missing support just may be the missing link that allows us to demystify why women make abortion decisions.

A Life Worth Sacrificing

The second category of women most at risk for abortion is those who have adopted a modern sense of self. Tracing back to the sexual revolution, we can spot the ways culture at large has evolved to think about the concept of self. In the book, *Strange New World: How Thinkers and Activists Redefined Identity and Sparked the Sexual Revolution*, Carl R. Trueman credits American scholar Robert Bellah for coining the term "expressive individualism," which is defined as the belief that "each person has a unique core of feeling and intuition that should unfold or be expressed if individuality is to be realized."[2]

This is considered the normative modern notion of selfhood in the West. One acts outwardly in accordance with one's inward feelings. Expressive individualism focuses on personal satisfaction as the meaning of life. Consequently, if an unplanned pregnancy will hinder one's personal satisfaction, the objective truth of the humanity of the child or the vulnerability of the baby in the womb is irrelevant. The child becomes a life worth sacrificing on the altar of self-satisfaction. Trueman aptly captures the impact here:

> The impact of expressive individualism on how we think about life and liberty has been dramatic. Old notions such as the sanctity of life and importance of freedom of religion and speech have been transformed, even inverted, by this new, modern self. And all this is because the notion of happiness with which we now intuitively operate is one where a sense of personal, psychological well-being is central. We might say that happiness is for each of us first and foremost an individual thing, resting upon us being independent; all other relationships must serve the end or be seen as oppressive."[3]

Understanding this notion of the modern self can greatly inform the way we work and communicate with women seeking abortions.

"So What if Abortion Ends a Life?"

Cultural trends and beliefs are easy to observe on TikTok. I recently watched a disturbing TikTok video that perfectly exemplifies Trueman's point. In the video, a young woman holds her precious baby, maybe two months of age, and tells the child that she could have aborted her. She repeats, "I could have killed you, but I chose to let you live. Yes, I realize what I just said and I stand by it." The young mother continues to rant that motherhood is a choice. She says the word "kill" is fine, like using hand sanitizer to kill germs. She ends with a proclamation that all women should have a choice. Don't oppress her rights.

It was difficult to watch, but this is an important reality check for the pro-life movement. We once believed that if everyone understood that a fetus is a baby, we'd win. If an expectant mother could hear the heartbeat, she would understand that the child inside of her is a person with rights, then she'd never abort. Yet, these arguments have been won. Few debate that a fetus won't grow up to be a baby. They're choosing abortion anyway.

My eyes were opened wide to this reality in 2013. Pro-choice writer Mary Elizabeth Williams had just published a piece for *Salon* titled, "So What if Abortion Ends a Life?" In it, she explained how she "never wavered for a moment in the belief that I was carrying a life inside of me. I believe that's what a fetus is: a human life. And that doesn't make me one iota less solidly pro-choice."[4]

There it was. Right there in black and white. This wake-up call for a much-needed change in strategy couldn't have been any clearer.

Yes, we have done an effective job reminding everyone that life begins at conception. But, what if, like Mary Elizabeth Williams, that doesn't really matter to the women most likely to have an abortion?

Williams effortlessly leaps over the biggest hurdle intended to stop her from having an abortion. She created a brand new paradigm where all are free to choose for themselves what is to be valued and what's to be discarded. According to Williams, "A fetus can be a human life without having the same rights as the woman in whose body it resides. She's the boss. Her life and what is right for her circumstances and her health should automatically trump the rights of the nonautonomous entity inside of her." According to Williams, activists should embrace the truth that "all life is not equal."[5]

Williams concludes that she "would put the life of a mother over the life of a fetus every single time, even if I still need to acknowledge my conviction that the fetus is indeed a life, a life worth sacrificing."

Rather than being representative of some radical pro-choice fringe, Williams's views now describe the rhetoric being used by the nation's largest abortion advocates. There's a greater force at work here than the concept of personhood; few are confused as to whether or not the baby is alive. Trueman's "expressive individualism" aptly explains Williams's sentiment. The baby becomes a life worth sacrificing.

Pro-choice advocacy group Reproductive Freedom for All (formerly NARAL) created a video, *Comedians in Cars Getting Abortions*, featuring a woman saying that she was tired of her body incubating a "person."[6] Hillary Clinton once defended abortion by saying that the "unborn person" does not have any constitutional rights.[7] And a pro-choice activist wrote an article for the motherhood website, Romper, that said becoming a mother made her more pro-choice than ever.[8]

Despite the cultural rhetoric, I'm grateful for the presence of ultrasound machines at many of our pregnancy centers so that men and women can glimpse life in the womb. Good work has been done over the last four decades to answer arguments about when life begins. But our world has changed, and perhaps we need to accept the reality that understanding the baby is alive does not stop abortions anymore. We can no longer assume that when a woman understands her baby is alive, she will always make a life decision. That's not what the data or stories from our pregnancy centers tell us. Pregnancy center staff can attest to stories of women seeing fully formed babies on ultrasound screens yet choosing abortion anyway. Even with the advent of 4D ultrasound technology, fetal heart monitors, and stories of babies surviving birth at less than twenty-five weeks, over one million abortions will likely happen this year.[9] Instead, we need to acknowledge that the two powerful drivers in a woman choosing to abort her baby are her lack of support and this sense of modern self.

Women Don't Want Babies

Many may assume that another main reason a woman would want an abortion is because she doesn't want children. Perhaps she's decided not to have children, or not to have children yet, and so abortion is the most viable option. But according to a five-year survey of people who had at least one abortion, only 3 percent of women cite "not wanting children" as the reason why they chose abortion. Instead, the top reasons for choosing abortion were: not financially prepared (40 percent); not a good time (36 percent); an issue with their partner (31 percent); or needing to focus on other children (29 percent).[10]

You may notice that there is some overlap in that a woman may have chosen more than just one reason for her abortion. But you may also notice that these top reasons for a woman to choose abortion have everything to do with her not feeling supported, most notably by the father of the baby. Plus, 60 percent of women who have abortions already have other children,[11] further reinforcing this isn't about avoiding or delaying motherhood for many women. Instead, it's about a lack of support or fear that a new baby will be too much added financial, social, and emotional responsibility in a situation where they are already feeling unsupported, primarily by the father of the children.[12]

To stop abortion, we must understand the real reasons why women choose to have abortions. This will give us the compassion and grace to understand the decision. Without increasing our understanding and empathy, it's like yelling at a deaf person. We can try talking louder and louder, but ultimately, they won't hear us.

Felt Needs Require Felt Support

If missing support is a key driver behind abortion decisions, can't we procure better funding for expectant mothers and help change that paradigm? The answer to this is no. For women to choose life, they need more than just material or physical support. They need emotional and spiritual support and discernment to make a life-affirming decision. When Jesus restores people, He meets every one of these needs.

Romans 12:2 instructs to not be "conformed to this world, but be transformed by the renewal of your mind, that by testing you may discern what is the will of God, what is good and acceptable and perfect." The only way to reach and assist the women choosing abortion is to offer more than just material support. They need life transformation that is only available through the power of the Holy Spirit, which is why the church has a vital role in changing the landscape of abortion in this nation.

The question we should ask ourselves is how we can offer these types of support to women to help them choose life. How do we offer them hope and let them know they are not alone? A social services model of support isn't enough to address the felt needs of the woman making an abortion decision.

We can relate to this concept. Every day we make decisions based on our felt needs. You drive through McDonald's because you're hungry. You wear a coat outside because you're cold. Our felt needs drive us on a primal level. It's almost instinctive. Our brains are designed to keep us alive; accordingly, our felt needs are going to win the day.

Similarly, the woman sitting on the table at Planned Parenthood isn't making a rational, well-thought-out decision from her prefrontal cortex. In most cases, she is having a stress-induced, fight-or-flight moment where she feels like she's deciding to save herself. It feels like the only viable option.

Though celebrity abortion advocates and the media paint a picture of women being rescued from oppression through abortion, this doesn't match the data. Here in the United States, the circumstances that lead to a woman's unplanned pregnancy and subsequent abortion remain with her long after her baby dies.

The pro-choice community ignores this reality. Abortion defenders have long treated the issue as one solely of a woman and her immediate choice to terminate her pregnancy. In this, they perform a great disservice to the woman, the father of the child, and their unborn baby. Women facing difficult pregnancy decisions are not given the help they need to see beyond their immediate situation into the possible ramifications of their decisions.

Abortion may eliminate the baby, but not the poverty, sexual abuse, and relationship difficulties the mother faces that often lead to her being at risk of abortion. Once her abortion is complete, the abortion clinic's services and assistance end. Abortion becomes like a financial transaction. You pay the clinic to "fix" this specific problem. Kind of like getting your transmission replaced or your water heater fixed. Abortion providers cannot offer the life transformation that so many women who seek abortions desperately need.

To this end, pro abundant life supporters have the opportunity to confront the realities of unplanned pregnancy and abortion head-on with their messaging. To do this most effectively we must stop agreeing with the pro-choice movement that abortion is solely a women's issue. This has been another great "aha" on my journey to a pro abundant life perspective. We can take things a step further and find a more winsome and holistic argument that will move our cause forward.

CHAPTER FOUR

WHY ABORTION IS NOT JUST A WOMEN'S ISSUE

When I describe Care Net's work, I love to tell the story of the woman at the well. In John chapter 4, Jesus meets a Samaritan woman at a well on the edge of town during the hottest part of the day. Typically, a woman would be at the well with other women of the town during the cooler part of the day, but she was there at noon all by herself. Christ, who knows us better than we know ourselves, knew that she was alone, that she had five husbands, and was currently living with a man who was not her husband. As a Samaritan woman in that culture, she would have been a social outcast.

Nevertheless, Christ offers her the living water of eternal salvation. Overwhelmed by His message and grace, she tells others in the town what happened. As a result of her testimony, many more Samaritans were saved. It's a beautiful story of Christ offering compassion, hope, and help to someone who was probably not accustomed to receiving any of those things. He meets her at her point of need, and she accepts His help and is saved.

Christ restores her spiritually, emotionally, and socially. I liken this to the work we do at Care Net. Facing a pregnancy decision, a woman comes to us for help. Like the woman at the well, many of these women have a "no-husband" problem causing them to consider abortion. As we discussed in the last chapter, lack of support now or in the future is the number one reason why a woman chooses to have an abortion. Following Christ's model, we have an opportunity. We can minister to these women spiritually, emotionally, and socially. We hope they will accept the compassion and choose life for their unborn child, and abundant life for themselves and their families.

Sexual Freedom and the Rise of Abortion Rights

Motherhood, fatherhood, and marriage were not always disconnected concepts in our society. Only a few years ago it would have been unthinkable to eliminate the need for fathers by discounting their relevance in the family.

Before *Roe v. Wade* was decided in 1973, abortion advocates spread the message that abortion rights were about the woman and the "product of conception." Gradually the message shifted to become about her and her choice. Then, it was about a woman and her "bodily autonomy."

The pro-life advocates countered that by insisting, "No, it's about the baby. We must save the baby." Pro-choice folks turned the attack toward us by saying we don't care about the woman, just saving babies. We countered, again, "It's about the woman *and* the baby. Love them both." And this is how the issue is currently framed by many in the pro-life movement.

I believe this is the wrong paradigm.

A reporter once asked me if Care Net was more for the woman or for the baby. "That's like asking me if I am more for breathing in or breathing out. They are both essential for life," I said.

We should object to abortion for two reasons—not just one. Not just because it's an assault on the sanctity of life, but also because it's an assault on the sanctity of marriage and family that God designed—fathers and mothers united in marriage loving each other and their children.

2 REASONS We Should Object to Abortion	**1** Assault on the Sanctity of Marriage and Family
	2 Assault on the Sanctity of Human Life

God's divine design for marriage and family stand diametrically opposed to the goals of the sexual revolution and abortion culture. God's design for the family has been all but obliterated in our culture. When the Supreme Court made abortion the law of the land, two things happened and we only talked about one—abortion. But this ruling did something new and destructive. It disconnected motherhood and fatherhood in the womb. From a legal perspective, motherhood begins at conception, but fatherhood begins at birth. It is difficult to engage men not married to the mother of the children during the first nine months of pregnancy because culture has told them they are not yet fathers. This disconnection creates perverse incentives for many men to avoid the responsibilities of fatherhood (and marriage) by pressuring women to abort. After all, rights and responsibilities are connected.

Care Net operates a Pregnancy Decision Line (PDL), which engages women and men at risk for abortion. One evening a male caller revealed just how deeply the disconnection between conception and fatherhood is ingrained in our culture. As our PDL coach attempted to discuss the situation with the man, he kept repeating that he did not want to be a father. But in reality, he was already a father, because like motherhood, fatherhood begins at conception. The question was what kind of father would he be—a father with a dead baby he helped to kill or a father with a live baby he helped to save. Interestingly, one thing driving this father to seek abortion was that his father had abandoned him, and he was terrified he would be this type of father too. Abortion is the ultimate abandonment of a vulnerable child because there is no chance for reconciliation this side of eternity. The only way he could avoid becoming his father was to do everything in his power to save his baby from abortion.

On the other side of the equation, committed fathers who want to take responsibility for their unborn children have little agency in our culture, and too often are discouraged from getting involved in the pregnancy. This is especially problematic since women at risk for abortion often cite the lack of their partner's emotional and financial support as a reason to end the pregnancy.

For champions of sexual freedom, this detachment was vitally necessary. The possibility of children threatened the unencumbered sexual lifestyle sought by the sexual revolution. Contraception was not always effective or utilized, so the possibility of pregnancy hampered the movement. During the 1960s and 70s, societal pressure meant that unplanned pregnancy usually resulted in marriage.

Goodbye sexual freedom.

This is why the sexual revolution's leadership called for abortion. Their revolution could have no "victory" without it. Almost fifty years after *Roe*, our culture still reels from the unlinking of marriage, motherhood, father-hood, sex, and pregnancy. While *Roe's* advocates argued that legalized abortion would reduce the number of out-of-wedlock births, instead the figure has skyrocketed.[1] So has the number of single-mother homes, which tend to be the poorest homes in the nation.[2]

The pro-choice movement has framed abortion as a women's issue for precisely this reason—it isolates the woman. Ironically, this isolation is viewed as empowerment. Women-centered messaging reinforces this narrative despite the reality that a woman at risk for abortion truly needs support from the father of her child, her family, the church, and her community.

A holistic, pro abundant life message surrounds rather than isolates a woman, both rhetorically and programmatically, with the loving support she needs to consider alternatives to abortion. Likewise, it limits the odds of her becoming a repeat client of either an abortion clinic or a life-affirming alternative, such as a pregnancy center.

Why are Planned Parenthood and other abortion influencers so set on men not being involved in the decision? Because he is a key influencer in the decision.

Men and the Abortion Decision

Care Net conducted a large national survey of women who have had an abortion.[3] We asked them, "Who did you talk to about your abortion decision, and who was the most influential?" We gave a long list of choices, including her mother, best friend, doctor, and even the abortion provider. The father of the baby was the most selected option. Frankly, it was not even close. The father of the baby is by far the most influential factor in a pregnancy decision.

Another large national survey conducted by Care Net asked men who had participated in abortion, "Who did she talk to about the abortion decision?" We gave them the same list that we gave to the women. The number one answer? "Me!" Then we asked who was the most influential in her decision to abort. Again, the man voted for himself. He said he was the most influential and knew he played a powerful role in her abortion decision.

I was not surprised by the survey results because I lived that scenario. For the first five months of Yvette's pregnancy, the only person on the planet who knew was me. It was clearly Yvette's choice whether to have an abortion or not. But do you think I was the key influencer? You bet I was! When I said I would be a husband to her and a father to our child growing inside of her, she could rest in the assurance that she had the physical, emotional, social, and spiritual support she needed to carry the baby to term and give him an abundant life.

In Care Net's 2021 survey of over one thousand men whose partners had abortions, we found that 31 percent did not give any advice at all and 61 percent were ready to "support her either way."[4] So the women who had abortions admit the father was most influential. And the men who participated in abortion said they know they were the most influential. This data changed my perspective. How could it not?

When I started working at Care Net back in 2012, I asked the hard and uncomfortable question that few in the pro-life movement were asking: Why are we not reaching the guy? It is her body and her choice legally and practically, but he's a key influencer. If you go back to the biblical narrative of the nativity, God proactively sought Joseph and called him to be a husband to Mary and a father to the Christ child growing inside of her. God sent an angel to help him understand his call and give him the confidence to accept it. I know from personal experience that's hard work.

Reach the Decision Makers

Early in my business career, I worked in sales and learned a few things about the most effective selling strategies. When faced with a sales situation, the most important thing is to identify both the decision maker and who influences the decision maker. I might meet with an executive, but oftentimes our conversation would uncover other stakeholders. "It's my business and my choice, but Joe in the back office advises me on everything we buy." I'd politely continue my conversation with the executive, of course. But the first opportunity I got I'd be outside Joe's office or calling him on the phone. If Joe is the key influencer that will make or break my sale, I want to talk to Joe. I have to get to Joe.

The same applies to Care Net. Our research shows men are key influencers, so part of our programming is specifically designed to reach them. These are pregnancy center programs designed specifically to invite men and fathers to be a part of the process.

You may be thinking, "That sounds great, but if a guy wants her to get an abortion, he's not interested in being a dad." I hear you. It's a real concern. But what if this is our opportunity to do God's work—to be the angel Gabriel to the men facing pregnancy decisions, who, like Joseph, are tempted to leave the women alone to face the consequences of an unplanned pregnancy?

First, we must understand the environment that a lot of these guys are in. We already discussed the statistics around father absence. And it's worth noting there's a confluence of these two social ills, abortion and father absence. If you're a man who grew up without a father, you might be terrified of being a father. The notion of stepping into that role would feel overwhelming. It's easier to run.

Culture reinforces this desire to run. For forty-plus years men have been fed the narrative that responsible men should say, "I support whatever decision you make," when she says she's pregnant. This cultural script has been beaten into guys' heads from every angle. Our survey showed 61 percent of post-abortive men responded in that manner.[5] Almost two-thirds of the men we talked to knew their lines. Right on cue.

But it's a terrible cultural script, and one that's like the messaging that says if you're a good man, you practice safe sex. But sex is not supposed to be safe in that way. It's the creation of one flesh that can bring life. That's a beautiful aspect of sex. So safe sex is a misnomer. Using a condom doesn't make sex safe. What God designed to be powerful and life-giving can't be tamed by a piece of latex. Yet the cultural narrative continues to beat two drums: safe sex and "I support you, whatever you decide."

This puts the weight of the decision back on the woman. She asks the baby's father, "What do I do?" A "pregnant pause" follows that often determines the trajectory of the life of the baby. If he says, "It's up to you, Babe," he abdicates his role as provider and protector. This script doesn't empower a woman. Instead, it leaves her feeling alone and unsupported. Who is most likely to get an abortion? The woman who is alone and unsupported.

Our culture touts this as a model for healthy masculinity. But nothing could be further from the truth. "Whatever you decide," is not masculinity. God made men to take responsibility for their actions.

CHAPTER FIVE

WHY FATHERS MATTER

When Mary faced an unplanned pregnancy (from her perspective, at least), the angel Gabriel delivered a message of abundant life. Mary had hopes and dreams for her life that did not include a baby at that time and in that way. Despite uncertainty about her future, she made a choice based on the certainty of what she did know: there was a life growing inside of her—a life worth protecting.

God's design for the sanctity of life, marriage, and family are intertwined in the birth story of Jesus Christ. Those who seek to protect the unborn should see this nativity narrative as an example consistent with God's design—a mother and father united in marriage loving their child and loving God.

From a human perspective, the story of Mary is a woman facing an unplanned pregnancy. Can you imagine how she felt when the angel told her she would conceive? Imagine the uncertainty swirling in her head. She had to wonder what her community would say. *How will you take care of this child?* She must have feared their shame and judgment. She also had to wonder what Joseph would say. *Will he believe me? Will he be angry?*

Mary was young and betrothed, which is a covenant marriage that had not been consummated. With her whole life in front of her, this was a giant interruption to her regularly scheduled life. Yet Mary focused on the certainty of what she knew instead of the uncertainty of what she didn't. When the angel gives her this overwhelming news she declares, "Let it be as to me, as you have said."

I like to think the work we do at Care Net encourages women to ascribe to the virtue and character of Mary—to tap into their "inner Mary," so to speak. We encourage women to focus on the certainty of what they do know, rather than the uncertainty of what they don't. We pray they understand there's a life growing inside, and it's not a life worth sacrificing, but a life worth sacrificing for.

Those on the other side of the issue want exactly the opposite. They want the woman to focus on the uncertainty of what she does not know. They want her to decide the future of her child based on this uncertainty. They want her to see the baby not as a life worth sacrificing for, but as a life worth sacrificing.

It's important to notice God made sure Mary's unplanned pregnancy wasn't a crisis pregnancy by sending an angel to comfort her. He also did something else that's critical for our understanding of the sanctity of the family. God sent an angel to Joseph.

Now Joseph was a man, and Joseph had a plan. (Because if you're a man without a plan, you ain't no kind of man!) Initially, Joseph had planned a "cultural abortion." He would put Mary and the unborn baby away quietly because back then you couldn't put the baby away as we do today with surgical and medical abortion. Every abortion-minded man facing an unplanned pregnancy should be able to relate to Joseph and his dilemma. Joseph's first instinct was to take the easier road and make it all go away quietly. But God intervened. He sent an angel to Joseph. That angel, Gabriel, called Joseph to be a husband to Mary and a father to the child growing inside of her. He chose life, too.

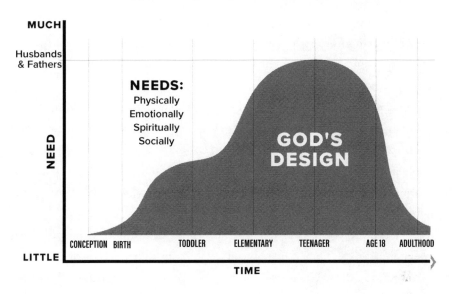

God could have orchestrated the birth and life of Christ so that Joseph was left out of the equation altogether. But he wasn't. Joseph played a crucial role in making sure Mary had the support she needed to raise Jesus. Technically, the Son of God would be the most well-equipped child to ever be raised by a single mom. But that's not the avenue God chose. Instead, He wants Joseph to be part of the story. Leading Joseph to his role as husband and father was a priority for God, and Joseph responded in faith and obedience. He didn't let his fear, doubts, or insecurities stop him from doing what God had asked.

Joseph v. Herod

God's plan for Joseph and his family takes an interesting turn when Jesus was born. It became a cage match of epic proportion, the likes of which you've never seen on UFC. It was a battle to see who was the GOAT: the greatest of all time.

At the time of Jesus's birth, Herod—who called himself Herod the Great—was the ruler. Herod was not in the line of David, but rather in the line of Esau. We know from Genesis 25 that Esau prioritized immediate pleasure. He sold his birthright to Jacob—his legacy, his future, and the awesome privilege and responsibility bestowed on the firstborn. He sold his own greatness for a bowl of soup.

As an ancestor of Esau, Herod the Great pursued greatness in the same shortsighted way as his forefathers. However, Herod was even worse. He sacrificed the vulnerable, even his own children, in his misguided pursuit of greatness. Herod, like Joseph, was faced with the news of an unplanned pregnancy. The difference is he responded by trying to kill Jesus. Herod wrote an edict ordering the murder of all boys under age two.

Herod didn't protect the vulnerable. He sacrificed the vulnerable. He worshipped the temporal in a misguided attempt to make himself eternal.

But Herod the Great really was no match for Joseph, husband, father, and righteous man. Joseph understood greatness comes not in sacrificing the vulnerable for yourself, but in sacrificing yourself for the vulnerable. And that's exactly what he did as a husband and as a provider.

Two paths are before us: the path of Herod or the path of Joseph. Joseph displays the perspective and spirit that we need today in men. He shows what it means to answer the call to God's mission. The holy family was a model for God's design for the family. That design for family could not happen without Joseph. Likewise, it can't happen today unless we engage dads.

Why Wasn't Jesus Born to a Single Mother?

God could have easily written the story in a way where Jesus was born to a single mother. The miracle of His birth would not have been any less significant. To bring Jesus into the world without Joseph may have accomplished God's purpose of bringing a Savior into the world, but it would've simultaneously violated God's design for families.

God intended children to come into the world with both a father and mother. God is the creator of this order. He is the divine designer. His plan is for a father and a mother to unite in marriage. They would love each other, love their child, and love God.

This was the order. And though Joseph didn't "father" Jesus, he became a father to Jesus so Jesus could come into the world in a way consistent with God's design. Mary and Joseph were already in a covenant relationship, a marriage that had not been consummated. So Jesus was born to an obedient, God-following couple covenanted to each other.

Solving for Missing Fathers

Considering that women choose abortion most frequently when they are isolated, alone, and unsupported, what situation changes a pregnant woman's level of support and isolation more than any other? Marriage.

This is what we should be solving for as much as possible when we think about the life issue. Now, don't hear me wrong. I'm not saying that for every woman who gets pregnant, she must marry every guy who got her pregnant. I understand that's not always realistic or the best solution. But we know the woman facing an unplanned pregnancy is in the dilemma because the two parties disconnected motherhood, fatherhood, sex, and marriage.

We also know when kids are raised by their two biological married parents, they tend to do better across every psychological, social, economic, and educational measurement of child well-being.

The Difference a Dad Makes

According to 2018 census numbers, 22.2 percent of all children in the United States under age 18 live in a home without their biological father.[1] That means one in every four children you meet is being raised without dad.

If we're just solving for "life" and our only concern is getting babies born, we're missing a big piece of the puzzle. We need to understand what happens when these babies are raised without their dads. Specifically, on average, children in father-absent homes are at risk for a range of intracta-ble social ills.[2] Outcomes are especially scary for boys being raised without their fathers. Boys raised in a home without their fathers are more likely to abuse alcohol and illegal substances. Family structure significantly impacts adolescent alcohol and substance use.[3] Boys with never-married mothers, stepfathers, and early divorce of parents had significantly greater rates of marijuana use.[4] Mental health and behavioral issues are also more common among boys raised in father-absent homes.

Moreover, researchers found that having a father in the household was associated with lower levels of aggression.[5] Similarly, the Millennium Co-hort Study assessed that children whose biological fathers stably joined the household had better cognitive and socio-emotional outcomes.[6]

Research also shows that children from two-parent families fare better in terms of their physical health. Researchers evaluated how lack of paternal involvement impacts infant mortality using a sample of 1,397,801 infants in Florida. Low father involvement increased infant mortality. Similarly, researchers concluded that high-quality interaction by any type of father predicted better infant health after a rigorous review of research on families and health published between 2000 to 2009.[7]

Children growing up with nonresident fathers are also most likely to live in unsafe neighborhoods. The results of the *Fragile Families and Child Wellbeing Study* indicated that children in single-mother households are more likely to live in impoverished communities with unemployment, crime, low-quality housing, poor health systems, poor education, and scant resourc-es.[8] According to data from 2011, children living in female-headed homes with no spouse present had a poverty rate of 47.6 percent. This was over four times the rate for children living in married-couple families.[9]

If our goal is simply to see the baby born, we are ignoring the wisdom and truth of scripture and the data showing children need their fathers.

The women most vulnerable to having an abortion are those who are struggling and unsupported. It's the woman already living in poverty, already trying to raise a child or children on her own. She doesn't know how she can emotionally or physically support another.

Sexual Activity/Teen Pregnancy Data

Promotion of responsible fatherhood could serve as an intervention strategy. Using data collected from 344 undergraduate students from psychology courses at two private universities, researchers learned that the earlier both males and females were no longer residing with their biological father, the more they engaged in casual sex and one-night stands.[10] Another study showed those whose fathers left after birth had first sex at younger ages than those with always-present fathers.[11] Among all the family processes, father involvement was the only factor that effectively decreased the odds of engaging in sexual activity. No other family processes were statistically significant.[12]

The safest situation for a baby to be born into and raised in is a two-parent home—one with both the mother and biological father present. Of course, this doesn't automatically mean all other situations are unsafe. We applaud responsible and generous stepdads who have tried to fill the gaps. Similarly, adoptive parents generously open their hearts and homes to provide a safe, secure, and loving environment for a child to be raised.

However, it's clear that without encouraging fathers to be involved, responsible, and committed, we are most likely setting single moms up for frustration and/or failure. Moreover, we will not have lasting success dealing with the abortion issue because we renew the cycle of early or uncommitted sex, unplanned pregnancy, and a single-mother household or abortion.

As people of the Book, it's our responsibility to communicate this high idea. "Loving them up" without connecting marriage, sex, and parenthood simply creates a repeat "customer." It happens too often. She'll be back—new guy and a new pregnancy. I call this the "18/18 Rule." We see this woman again in eighteen months and we see her daughter at risk for abortion in eighteen years or someone her son got pregnant in eighteen years. That's not ministry. That's a *transactional* consumer retail business, not a *transformational*, covenant-building, relationship-building ministry.

We can't let the low ideas of people degrade the magnitude of God's high ideas. Here's my case and point with a very personal example. I am a Black man, and if no one was committed to God's high ideas, I'd still be a slave today. Thomas Jefferson wrote in the Declaration of Independence, "we hold these truths to be self-evident, that all men are created equal." At that time, Jefferson held slaves. However, the Declaration of Independence was an aspirational document—a high idea. Though he was a flawed man, Jefferson had an aspirational perspective. He knew there was something morally wrong; it was wrong for one man to own another man. Jefferson wrote about an idea he hadn't yet personally been able to adopt. He did not let the "low ideas" he was living stop him from declaring the high ideas.

As a result, decades later Abraham Lincoln rallied the nation around these high ideas to end slavery. A few more decades later, Dr. Martin Luther King Jr. challenged the nation to end the sin of discrimination and Jim Crow. These great men challenged us to live up the promises of this high idea so that others who look like me can proudly declare, "Free at last! Free at last! Thank God Almighty, we are free at last!"

MINISTRY MOMENT   Q CARE NET

HOW CARE NET BEGAN REACHING MEN

In 2013, Care Net started a focused effort to reach the father of the baby at risk for abortion. The first resource developed was "Before She Decides," which was designed to encourage and equip the father of the baby to speak into the pregnancy decision the mother of the baby faced in a life-affirming way. Over time, additional resources and training were developed to help expand this key area of programming.

To further this critical work, in 2021 Care Net invested significant funding, resources, and training to launch ten pilot fatherhood programs at pregnancy centers around the country. Care Net used data from the pilot programs to improve procedures, and in 2023 we doubled the project size. Response from the initial program was so positive that ninety of our pregnancy centers applied to be part of the project expansion. We carefully selected ten more centers to roll out the expanded program. As part of their commitment, the centers collected data and recorded progress that indicated whether the program met benchmark goals.

One Care Net affiliate in Grand Rapids, Michigan, has this motto: "Show me a neighborhood where fathers are involved, and I will show you a neighborhood that is thriving." This is their rallying cry to serve fathers. Alpha Grand Rapids is pioneering a new form of fatherhood ministry, becoming the first in the nation with a stand-alone building to serve fathers. While this venture is only a few years old, many of the approaches they are taking are changing the game in the pregnancy care movement.

Alpha Men's Center has several signature programs intended to help men grow as partners, fathers, and community leaders. The Step-Up program provides dads with the opportunity to meet regularly with a trained volunteer—called a coach—in a one-on-one setting. Appointments are one hour long and may include conversations centered around parenting, health, relationships, and faith. Care Net's Doctor Dad® course helps new and expectant fathers learn how to care for their pregnant partners, what to expect during pregnancy and after birth, and how to tend to their baby's basic needs in sickness and in health. The program gives dad something to do to feel confident and equipped in caring for his child. Plus, the center runs fatherhood groups and offers job skills training.

Twenty years ago, few would have considered opening a men's center, but this model is working. The center has watched men choose life for their unborn children and, alongside their partners, accept Christ, learn new life skills, and find a supportive community as they work through struggles such as mental health issues or substance abuse. This is how we truly affect change: one father, one family, one neighborhood at a time.

CHAPTER SIX

WHY MARRIAGE IS CRITICAL TO END ABORTION

When I first started working at National Fatherhood Initiative in 2001, the goal seemed straightforward: encourage men to engage in the lives of their children. We promoted what we called "involved, responsible, and committed fatherhood."

We did great work engaging dads and helping them develop fathering skills to connect heart-to-heart with their children. We also went to places where dads were most likely to be disengaged from their children—like prisons—and taught them how to reconnect.

Yet there was one piece of data that loomed over every move we made, every initiative we started, and every program we launched. The absolute best way to ensure a child has a good relationship with his or her father is when the child's father and mother are married.

Though some may have thought we were moving away from a pro-fatherhood message when we began to stress the importance of married fatherhood, we saw this as the missing link. Marriage is the institution God designed for the betterment of children, women, and men. Yes, we live in a sinful, fallen world, and not every marriage is a healthy situation for everyone involved. But some have wrongly disregarded the entire *institution of marriage* and the benefits for adults and children because of the failings of some *individuals in marriage.*

Consider this illustration. Imagine if someone is driving and ends up in a ditch because they got distracted by checking text messages. What would you think if they said they would never drive again and declared that cars were not useful? Rightly, you would make a distinction between the car and the driver of the car. You would also point out that there are principles to good driving and when you follow these principles, a car generally does just fine and you stay on the road. Well, the same is true for marriage. When one follows the principles and behaves in marriage in the covenant context for which God designed it, marriages last for a lifetime.

That said, as I transitioned into ministry at Care Net, I soon saw the same missing link when it came to promoting and discussing the importance of marriage. As I scoured the data, engaged leaders in the pro-life movement, and witnessed the stories from our affiliated pregnancy centers and PDL hotline, I recognized the same truth applied. Unless the pro-life movement embraces the promotion of marriage, we're missing out on the great catalyst available to stop abortion. Emphasizing marriage is a source of greater hope and security for those children whose parents chose life, and it's the number one deterrent to abortion. In fact, my story is a perfect example. My wife Yvette and I never faced another abortion dilemma because we married.

Though some have tried to back away from the marriage message, possibly out of fear that promoting marriage would be a distraction to the cause of saving lives, this strategy is actually shortsighted. Marriage is central to the pro abundant life message because marriage is the place where abortions are least likely to happen.

Think about it. Let's say you're the chief of police in a city where crime is out of control. You've tried everything to bring your crime rates down, but nothing seems to work. There's a city, not too far away, that has a significantly lower crime rate. Wouldn't you try to find out what they're doing to reduce crime and replicate it in your city? Couldn't you potentially solve your own city's crime problem by identifying and replicating these best practices for making a city safe?

Similarly, the data is clear. Marriage is the safest place to raise children who will refrain from engaging in risky sexual behaviors that lead to unplanned pregnancies.[1] Likewise, the benefit of marriage for adults facing an unplanned pregnancy is unmatched in its ability to deter abortions. Remember, 87 percent of abortions are among unmarried women.[2] I believe that even the possibility of a high-quality and low-conflict marriage—when a woman believes a good marriage may be part of her near future—can act as a deterrent to an abortion decision.

Marriage is, without a doubt, the safest "city" for an unplanned pregnancy. Remember the results of the study we discussed earlier? The first person a pregnant woman tells is the father. The most influential person in her decision is the baby's father. The very act of her telling him and involving him in her decision reveals a hidden desire for many women. She wants him to step up and take responsibility for the unborn child she is carrying. She wants him to acknowledge that he had a part in this, and take ownership.

If she wasn't hoping for a life-affirming response from him, why tell him? Candidly, doing so could very well make things worse for her. He could tell others, including those she doesn't want to know. Or, worse, he could place other obstacles in her way.

Now, let me, again, be clear. As important as marriage is, a pro abundant life perspective does not mean that marriage is *always* the right decision for a couple. Some couples are in an unhealthy relationship where marriage would be unwise. But it does mean that we should always look for ways to help a couple move toward marriage, if possible.

The High Idea of Marriage

It may feel like a high idea—trying to promote and encourage marriage and family in a culture that's become increasingly hostile to the concept. In 2023, 47 percent of the US population was single. That's 117.6 million people who were either unmarried or divorced. In 1990, only 29 percent of the population was single. In 1960, fewer than seven million Americans lived alone.[3, 4]

Unless we focus on this high idea, unless we communicate the values of marriage and family, how will they be communicated to our children? How can the cycle be broken unless we teach our children God's design for the family? It's difficult to be what you don't see and model for your children what has not been modeled for you. A woman and a man who are facing an unplanned pregnancy have disconnected fatherhood, motherhood, sex, and marriage and God's design for those things. They've walked in the fullness of that dynamic, and the unplanned pregnancy is a consequence.

We don't let how other people are living determine our ability, willingness, and commitment to communicate high ideas. God's design for marriage and family is a high idea. Moreover, it's the idea and life choice with the most potential to protect the lives of the unborn.

Beyond Saving Babies

Even if the couple doesn't marry, we must help them relink marriage, motherhood, fatherhood, sex, and pregnancy. We need to change their worldview, connecting these things so that hearts and minds can be changed before their next sexual opportunity. Otherwise, we only create repeat clients—for either our pregnancy centers or the abortion clinics.

Furthermore, we must break the intergenerational abortion risk. We want parents who choose life to communicate and model God's design for sex and family, especially to children who do not live in a family structure that is modeling this design. As I think back to my own story, I didn't have many married male role models showing me what it meant to be a father and a husband. Mike Brady, from *The Brady Bunch*, and James Evans, from *Good Times*, may have been my most regular influence in this arena, but they were on television. As I think about what boys watch on television today, what they learn on YouTube, and the cultural influences they feel through social media and video games, this generation of boys isn't learning how to be husbands or fathers from key influencers in our culture. If they don't learn it at home (and from the church), they won't be able to see it, desire it, or replicate it.

We know that the best way to ensure children not only survive but thrive in life is when they are raised by their own two married parents. The pro-life movement cannot be satisfied with creating a generation of children raised in a single-mother home. That's like declaring victory at the end of the first half of the game even though your best players left the game with injuries.

Yes, we should certainly celebrate the saving of a life and the formation of a family.

Yes, we should certainly provide the new single mother and her child the support they need.

When a woman faced with an unplanned pregnancy commits to being a single mother, this is a courageous, life-affirming act. But is that really God's design, God's desire, or what God wants for mothers and children? I grew up in a single-mother home and I know well how difficult it can be for a mother and her children. In fact, I wrote a book called *Raising Sons of Promise: A Guide for Single Mothers of Boys* about growing up in this challenging family dynamic.

Indeed, decades of social science research shows us that children in unmarried or father-absent homes face significant challenges in life. If we don't strive for an approach more comprehensive than just saving babies to be raised in potentially challenging environments that will, according to the data, perpetuate generational repetition of these same challenges, then we are giving ammunition to our opponents.

Pro-choice advocates can assess the data and argue that "the child would have been better off never having been born." From a biblical perspective, it's easy to disagree. But unless we do more than just "get the baby born," we are paving the way for precious new lives to be in scenarios that are less safe and secure than what God intended. When the pro-life movement leaves marriage and fatherhood out of the conversation, we help create situations that we've spent decades trying to reduce: the intergenerational cycle of abortion, unwed childbearing, father absence, and the breakdown of the family.

Instead, we should embrace the truth. Remember the data? Children in father-absent homes are two to four times more likely to live in poverty, use drugs, drop out of school, be abused or neglected, be obese, become incarcerated, and have emotional or behavioral problems. They are more likely to be sexually active and, therefore, more at risk for abortion.

The work of the pro abundant life movement doesn't end when the baby's life is saved from abortion—it begins there. *Bios* life is only part of the equation. The work of providing parenting, relationship and financial support, and marriage education to parents who have chosen life must be fully integrated into every aspect of the pro-life movement.

As compelling as the reasons are for focusing on marriage to address the issues and difficulties an unplanned pregnancy presents, there is a key reason that trumps them all. It's what God did.

When Mary faced an unplanned pregnancy, (from her perspective), God sent an angel to Joseph. The first thing the angel told Joseph was to not be afraid to take Mary as his wife—affirming the sanctity of marriage and family as God designed. Since the order of communications matters in Scripture, one would expect the angel to first tell Joseph to protect the Christ child growing in Mary's womb—affirming the sanctity of life. But this is not what happened, and this fact is essential to fully embracing the pro abundant life approach, which is modeled for us by God in the first chapter of the first book of the New Testament.

God accomplished his purpose to bring the Christ child into the world without violating his principal blueprint—the high idea—of how he desires all children to come into the world, with a mother and father, united in marriage, loving their child and loving God. Indeed, the holy family was wholly family. As exemplified by Jesus's birth story and corroborated by reams of social science data, we cannot separate the sanctity of life from the sanctity of marriage and family without consequences. So, as pro abundant life people, we should "go and do likewise" in our response to the abortion issue.

PART TWO:

GOD'S CALL TO DISCIPLESHIP

CHAPTER SEVEN

WHY THE CHURCH MUST LEAD ON THE ABORTION ISSUE

A few years ago, I had the honor to speak about the life issue at a church. At the end of the service, I stood outside of the sanctuary to greet some of the congregants. As I was speaking to one woman, I noticed a young man out of the corner of my eye. He had a sheepish look on his face, and I could tell he was waiting for the others to leave to speak to me.

Once they did, he approached me and the first thing he said was, "I appreciated your remarks, but I wished I'd heard them last Sunday, because this week I took my girlfriend to have an abortion."

Regret was plainly written all over his face. My heart went out to him. It struck me that his face probably looked like Judas's face when he sought to return the thirty pieces of silver. Like this young man, Judas had essentially "aborted" Jesus—he wrongly and unjustly sacrificed an innocent life for his own benefit.

Like Judas, this young man was a Christ follower. He considered himself to be deeply pro-life, participated in the national March for Life, and often debated people who did not share his pro-life conviction. He was deeply pro-life…*until he wasn't*.

I won't share all the details of what he said to me, except this: He strongly influenced his Christian girlfriend to have an abortion, drove her to the abortion clinic, and sat in the waiting room while they took the life of his child.

As I spent time processing this interaction, it became even clearer to me that we have a significant issue with abortion in the church. Too many Christ followers are in the church on Sunday and the abortion clinic on Monday. Alas, the pro-life movement has spent a great amount of time and resources trying to reach those far from Jesus with one clear message: that an unborn baby is a life. But have we missed our own? Are we trying to gain the whole world while losing the souls in our congregations?

This reality was a pivotal part of my journey to the pro abundant life position. Our message is centered on the truth that lasting change is not found only in intellectually proving abortion's harm on women, men, and their children—it is found in the person of Jesus Christ. Any message of life that misses Jesus is incomplete and short-lived. If we can't convince Christians not to get abortions, how can we expect to be successful with those who are far from Christ?

A Wake-Up Call for the Church

Intellectual arguments or religious exposure are not enough to prevent a couple from choosing abortion. After nearly fifty years of providing compassion, hope, and help to clients at its network of affiliated pregnancy centers, Care Net has found that too often the social and situational pressures to abort can thwart even our most compelling arguments to choose life.

In my twelve years with Care Net, I've walked the halls of our affiliated pregnancy centers and spent hours talking to the caring and compassionate people who steadfastly minister daily to women and men at risk for abortion. Many have privately shared with me that their Christian clients are among their most challenging. These women and men know what's right. They know that a baby is a life. They know what choice they should make. And, yet, they are making the wrong decision more often than one would expect given their professed faith in Jesus Christ.

Look at this alarming data. In two national Care Net studies, four out of ten women and five out of ten men who have had abortions were attending church *at least once a month* at the time of their first abortion.[1,2] According to the Guttmacher Institute, 54 percent of women who have abortions identify as either Protestant or Catholic.[3] To see the impact of this reality, consider that there are more than one million abortions a year. If 40 percent are to Christian women, that's four hundred thousand. Abortion typically costs about five hundred dollars or more. So, this would mean that Christians are spending about 200 million dollars a year on abortions at the same time Christians are marching to stop it.

So, this would mean that Christians are spending about 200 million dollars a year on abortions at the same time Christians are marching to stop it.

Simply getting Christians to stop having abortions would have a significant impact on the number of lives we save every year. This is a log in our eye and there is an urgent need to overturn the desire for abortion in our own pews.

To suggest that we have a significant and troubling issue of abortion within the Christian church is not an overstatement. My question is this: what kind of circumstances lead a woman who knows that abortion is wrong to do it anyway? We've already discussed the hows and whys. These are no different for a woman who claims to be a Christian. When she feels alone, when she's unmarried and unsupported, and when she can't see a vision for her life that includes the kind of support she'd need to raise a baby, abortion feels like a more viable alternative than life.

And that's why the church must hear this alarm bell sounding. The church has a unique role in the abortion paradigm. Remember that statistic? Forty percent of the women who had an abortion were in church at least once a month. I'm hard-pressed to name another place where we can reach 40 percent of women having abortions, where we can also meet them where they are, speak into their lives, and disciple them. I can't think of one.

The problem is that these men and women are sitting in our pews, but they aren't being transformed. Why? Because too many pastors avoid talking about issues of life completely for fear that it sounds "too political." While I appreciate the sensitivity, issues like poverty, homelessness, and hunger have a political component, but I have never heard a pastor say he would not speak about these issues. The bottom line is that if we don't start offering clear, biblical teaching on why choosing life is necessary, we will continue to lose ground. We cannot win in any of the arenas where we are trying to fight abortion without the unwavering and consistent leadership of pastors and the support of the church.

Now, don't get me wrong. There are many churches out there preaching about life. The church has spent decades anchored on the argument that choosing life is best because scripture teaches us not to murder. But, as we've already discussed, this isn't the heart of an abortion decision for many men and women. There's no longer the same confusion, perhaps, regarding whether abortion was taking a life. The science is clear, but abortion decisions aren't black and white for many.

Along my journey to understand issues of abortion and life through the lens of scripture, the Holy Spirit has shown me another angle—another way to frame the abortion issue that can help men and women better understand the importance of these issues from a biblical perspective. Specifically, as Christians, we must see how the abortion issue is divinely connected to our two most fundamental mandates directly from Christ: the Great Commandment and the Great Commission.

Two Bookends: The Great Commandment and the Great Commission

As Christians, we're called to live out two great initiatives in our private lives: the Great Commandment and the Great Commission. These two bookends of the Christian faith represent Christ's call to all of us, and we are charged to promote and boldly proclaim them in the public square.

The Great Commandment is found in the Gospel accounts of Matthew, Mark, and Luke. I especially like the discussion in Luke 10:25–37 because a lawyer comes to Jesus. Given the legal context of today's abortion debate, this is rather ironic. In any case, this lawyer asked Jesus, "What shall I do to inherit eternal life?" Of course, Jesus didn't dismiss the question, because it's one that everyone should be asking. Instead, He leaned into the question because He thought it was a good one. He responded, "What is written in the Law?"

The lawyer responded, "You shall love the Lord your God with all your heart and with all your soul and with all your strength and with all your mind, and your neighbor as yourself." Jesus gives him the thumbs up—this is the Great Commandment. In other parts of scripture, Jesus teaches how all of scripture hangs on these truths.

Three Loves

The Great Commandment rests on three loves: love of God, love of neighbor, and love of self. Reflecting on this in the context of the life issue and abortion, God gave me an amazing insight about the word "neighbor." In Greek, it means "near one" or "near fellow." So loving your neighbor as yourself means "loving your near one as you love yourself."

When you look at the word "love" used in this verse, it is the highest love possible. In Greek, it is *agapē*, or agape love in English. It is a sacrificial love. This same word for love is used in John 3:16, "For God so *loved* the world, that he gave his only Son, that whoever believes in him should not perish but have eternal life." It's also used in John 15:13, "Greater *love* has no one than this, that someone lay down his life for his friends." The Great Commandment says the type of love we are supposed to have for our neighbors, our near ones, is sacrificial.

How does this relate to the life issue? If a woman is pregnant, who is her nearest "near one"? Nearness can be considered in two ways—physical proximity and relationship proximity. Think "next of kin." In the case of a pregnant woman, it is her baby growing in her womb. Her baby is as physically and relationally close to her as possible.

Now, for the man who got a woman pregnant, who is his near one? In this context, the vulnerable woman certainly is his neighbor. But the baby in her womb—bone of his bone and flesh of his flesh—is his nearest near one, his next of kin. Whether we profess to be pro-life or pro-choice, we must, as Christians, ask ourselves how the decision to abort a baby, one of God's image bearers, is an act of sacrificial love toward God?

More succinctly, how does aborting a child align with the Great Commandment? Remember, Jesus said this commandment is the first and greatest: to love God and to love your neighbor as yourself. So, abortion is a violation of the Great Commandment.

We must then ask ourselves a second question. How is aborting your near one, this baby in the womb, an act of sacrificial love for your neighbor? There are three inseparable loves in this passage—love for God, love for neighbor, and love for self. If you separate these loves, the virtue of the Great Commandment can become a vice.

For example, if one loves God but does not love his neighbor, that's a problem because 1 John 4:21 declares, "And this commandment we have from him: whoever loves God must also love his brother." If one loves his neighbor and his self but does not love God, that's humanism. Moreover, one's love for neighbor is not anchored in anything immutable. It's like a boat tied to another boat, but not to a dock. Things are fine until the storms and challenges of life come and your neighbor's boat starts pulling you into rough water. In those cases, we tend to cut the rope, don't we? With humanism, our neighbors can easily become lives worth sacrificing.

And finally, we must ask the third question. How is having an abortion an act of love for self? Of course, the pro-choice culture says it is. But this is a deception for a number of reasons. First, in Matthew 18:6, Christ boldly declares the primacy of protecting vulnerable children when he says it's better to go swimming with a millstone on your neck than to hurt a child. So, the act of abortion creates antipathy between God, the creator of life, and those who destroy innocent life. Putting oneself at odds with an almighty God is certainly not an act of loving oneself.

I can attest to countless stories of women and men who have struggled with past regrets for abortion decisions. Care Net has a key ministry outreach called Abortion Recovery and Care (ARC) designed to help post-abortive women and men. When the abortion decision is made, there is often a rush of relief and regret is low. But as time passes, regret emerges as the realization sets in that one has taken an innocent human life. I call this dynamic the Relief/Regret Cross Over.

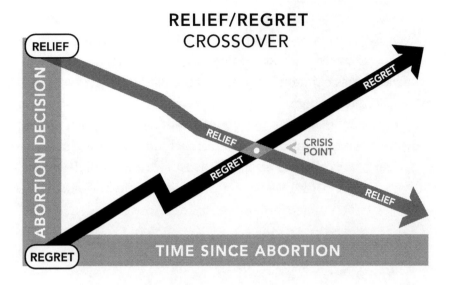

Women and men are often haunted for decades with guilt and shame from regret that requires deep spiritual healing. Anyone who truly loves themselves would avoid the spiritual despair and emotional trauma in the aftermath of an abortion.

Indeed, abortion is an act that declares from its core, "I don't love God and I don't love my neighbor, but I do love myself." This type of self-love becomes the vice of idolatry. The sacrificial love for others that Jesus calls us to in the Great Commandment becomes a sacrificing love for self—the vulnerable little one in the womb becomes a child sacrifice. A life worth sacrificing, not a life worth sacrificing for. The virtue becomes a vice.

CARE NET'S ABORTION CARE AND RECOVERY

The mission of Care Net's Abortion Recovery and Care (ARC) program is to connect, equip, and support those seeking abortion recovery. According to two Care Net surveys conducted through Lifeway Research, five of ten men and four of ten women were attending church regularly at the time of their abortion. Accordingly, churches across our nation are filled with post-abortive women and men. Care Net connects women and men impacted by abortion with individual ministries, pregnancy centers, and churches that provide healing resources. This approach equips individuals and organizations to provide abortion recovery through Bible studies and other training. Care Net also fosters community building where hope in Christ and healing from abortion is possible.

The Story of the Good Samaritan

Back in the book of Luke where Jesus lays out the Great Commandment, the lawyer responds to Jesus by asking, "So who is my neighbor?"

The lawyer, realizing he is called to a sacrificial love, tries to narrow the scope. It's much like when Peter asked Jesus, "How many times shall I forgive my brother or sister who sins against me?" (Matthew 18:21 NIV). Sometimes as Christians, we are tempted to minimize a higher calling when we are face to face with it. We ask questions like, "How little do I need to do to get into heaven?" Jesus didn't simply answer the lawyer's question. As is typical of Jesus, He answered a question with a story—the Good Samaritan.

He describes what happens when a vulnerable person, at risk and unable to advocate for himself, is injured by robbers and left on the side of the road to die. A priest comes by, but moves to the other side of the road to distance himself from the messy (in their time, unclean) situation. Later, a Levite does the same. But when a Samaritan comes along, he draws close to the dying man, binds his wounds, and takes him to an inn. He cares for the vulnerable person with a sacrifice of time, talent, and treasure.

The "people of the Book," the priest and the Levite, moved far from the near one—their neighbor. Essentially, they "aborted" him in his time of vulnerability. Of course, they had their reasons—spiritual, ministry-related, political, and maybe even social justice reasons. But their reasons didn't align with biblical justice, which requires sacrificial love for the vulnerable. The Samaritan's act shows us the pursuit of righteousness (which should have been the focus of the priest and Levite) must be linked to the pursuit of justice and mercy if we are to truly live out the agape love required by the Great Commandment.

After Jesus tells the story, He asks the lawyer, "Which of these three do you think was a neighbor to the man who fell into the hands of robbers?" The lawyer replies, "The one who had mercy on him." Then Jesus instructs, "Go and do likewise" (Luke 10:36-37 NIV). In other words, be a neighbor to your neighbor.

The Mercy of the Womb

A look at the etymology of Hebrew words further bolsters the beauty of this story. The Hebrew root for the words "mercy" and "compassion" is the same root as the word for "womb." The Good Samaritan put this vulnerable person in a "womb." We are called to model his example by showing sacrificial love to our neighbors.

The womb of a mother is a place of mercy. It's also a point of vulnerability that we share with every person who has ever lived. The only language that babies in the womb have to express themselves is their heartbeats, and I believe that every baby's heartbeat says, "Have mercy…Have mercy…Have mercy." And every time a mother hears that heartbeat, she hears, "Have mercy…Have mercy…Have mercy."

If you're reading this, your mother responded, like the Good Samaritan, with agape love. A sacrificial love that says our lives were worth sacrificing for. The only reason any of us are here today is because our mothers, Christian or not, followed the principle of the Great Commandment as it relates to pregnancy.

When you look at the life issue through the lens of the Great Commandment, you see a uniquely Christian, pro abundant life apologetic straight from the mouth of Jesus. Whether it's human trafficking, food security, helping the incarcerated, or caring for the poor, the Great Commandment is the standard we must use to direct our actions for every issue. For Christians who profess to be pro-choice, they must reconcile their perspective with the Greatest Commandment of Jesus himself.

The Great Commission

The other bookend of our call as Christians is the Great Commission, found in Matthew 28:19–20. The Great Commission calls us to "make disciples of all nations, baptizing them in the name of the Father and of the Son and of the Holy Spirit, teaching them to observe all that I have commanded you." Thankfully, Jesus made this simple when he said of the Great Commandment, "On these two commandments depend all the Law and the Prophets" (Matthew 22:40). In other words, we are to live out the

> *...we are to live out the Great Commandment in order to fulfill the Great Commission.*

Great Commandment in order to fulfill the Great Commission.

We are called to make disciples. But who are the folks we are supposed to disciple so they, in turn, can learn to follow Jesus and go disciple others? The answer: our neighbors. Our near ones. Every parent's first discipleship calling is their children. For Christians professing to be pro-choice, I ask this question. How is aborting their children—those who they are to make disciples of Jesus Christ—an act of disciple making?

This is the equivalent of missionaries going to a foreign land to make disciples and then sacrificing them so the missionaries can have better lives for themselves. Unfortunately, this was a common criticism of some early missionary efforts. Their "disciple making" consisted of subjugating and even killing those they were called to love sacrificially.

As I hope you'll agree, it's clear that the act of abortion is a violation of the Great Commandment and a violation of the Great Commission, both callings to all followers of Christ.

If churches adopted an approach to the abortion issue that centers solely on the teaching of Jesus, any fears of this topic being "too political" for the pulpit should be alleviated.

Where Mr. Rogers Meets Big Bird

The concept of combining the Great Commandment and the Great Commission—loving and discipling our "near ones"—is where Mr. Rogers meets Big Bird.

While Mr. Rogers asked his young viewers, "Won't you be my neighbor?" Big Bird and his *Sesame Street* friends sang, "Who are the people in my neighborhood?" As followers of Christ, we can recognize that our neighbors are our near ones. And, we can hear the cry of the unborn baby in the womb beckoning, "Won't you be my neighbor?" We must also make sure that our "neighborhoods," as *Sesame Street* characters explain, include and don't sacrifice the most vulnerable. Indeed, no one, except Oscar, wants to end up in a trash can!

Part of Jesus's point in the story of the Good Samaritan and the principles of both the Great Commission and the Great Commandment is to make our neighborhoods wider—to define our neighbors as anyone God sets before our paths to love, care for, or disciple.

Furthermore, we must bear in mind the Great Commandment and Great Commission are integral to God's plan for mankind because they are evident in the garden of Eden. In the second chapter of Genesis, Adam did not have a neighbor and could not live out the Great Commandment. God said it was not good for Adam to be alone, and remedied the situation by making a helper.

So, God created Eve. He could have created Eve from the dust just like Adam. But remember the Great Commandment says to love your neighbor as yourself. Therefore, God created Eve from Adam's rib—his own self. She had a unique connection and intimacy with Adam that foreshadowed a woman carrying a baby in the womb. The baby is part of her, but it is a separate and distinct living human being with a unique destiny and purpose ordained by God.

If God told Adam to love his neighbor as himself, he would look at his side and look at Eve. And if God told Eve to love her neighbor as herself, she would look at herself and then look at Adam's side. So, Adam and Eve in the garden of Eden were living out the Great Commandment—to love God and to love their neighbors as themselves.

Adam and Eve were given a mandate to be fruitful and multiply to fill the earth. In other words, they were called to have children. And they were going to teach their children all that God taught them—how to love each other and to only eat from the tree of life. Like the calling of every Christian parent today, Adam and Eve were going to make disciples of their children. Before sin entered the garden of Eden, Adam and Eve were living out the Great Commandment to fulfill the Great Commission.

Adam and Eve's offspring continue the spiral. When Cain kills Abel, it's clear that Adam and Eve have failed to fulfill the Great Commission to disciple their son as a follower of the Great Commandment. Cain was called to be his brother's keeper and sacrificially love him in the same way that a woman who conceives a baby and a man who facilitates the conception are called to be their neighbor's keeper and sacrificially love their child.

Understanding the centrality of the Great Commandment and the Great Commission as a Christian response to the abortion issue is an important distinction between being pro abundant life and just being pro-life. Again, you can be an atheist and be pro-life (focused on *bios*) but you can't be pro abundant life (focused on *bios* and *zoe*). Many people hold a pro-life perspective, but it is not anchored in these essential commandments from the mouth and example of Jesus. Indeed, one's perspective may be anchored to a parent's beliefs or conviction they held as a teen, but when they face a crisis—when the issue comes home to their neighborhood—that's when their beliefs get put to the test. That's when one's pro-life perspective must be concretely connected to a biblical worldview.

This perspective gave Jesus an unwavering commitment in the garden of Gethsemane when tremendous pressure mounted to abort the mission the Father had given Him. Jesus's death on the cross was the final act in His humanity to live out the Great Commandment, sacrificially loving His beloved neighbors, to fulfill the Great Commission that we might become disciples who make disciples who live and love like He did.

Why you are pro-life matters. A lot. This is why using the term pro abundant life makes everything we believe about life and scripture even clearer. When someone asks why you are so committed to protecting little ones in the womb, your answer must be that to do otherwise would be a violation of the Great Commandment and the Great Commission.

The Church's Opportunity and Calling

There's a critical need for churches to minister to the abortion vulnerable. Several years ago, Care Net research found most women who had abortions did not feel their church had any resources to help with their unplanned pregnancy decisions.[4] Others feared judgment from the congregation should they find out about the pregnancy. Remember, Care Net's large national study of women who had abortions found four out of ten women were attending church at least once a month when they had their first abortion.

Sanctity of Human Life Sunday was established to encourage pastors to talk about abortion and inspire their congregations to create a culture of life inside and outside the church. Despite the abortion issue being the most consequential life and death situation our nation faces, many pastors don't incorporate that event into their sermons or teaching. Nor do their churches have a viable and compelling ministry response to offer compassion, hope, and help for those at risk for abortion. Most of the women we surveyed didn't believe their pastors were talking about this issue at all. Despite pro-life efforts to mobilize the church, abortion remains a taboo subject for too many pastors. Some say it's too "political" and others say it's too "controversial."

When pastors don't address the abortion issue, it becomes easier for a woman at risk for abortion to believe she will be treated like the woman caught in adultery if she discloses her dilemma to her church. She may feel that she will be stoned with condemnation. We must be mindful that we cannot stone the woman without stoning the vulnerable baby she carries inside her.

We need a new approach to abortion in the church, one grounded in scripture and pastoral ministry so we can truly engage and mobilize both pastors and congregants to offer compassion, hope, and help to women and men at risk for abortion inside and outside the church. Though *Roe v. Wade* has been overturned in the court, the church has a specific challenge to overturn *Roe v. Wade* in its pews and in the broader culture.

Absolutes, Convictions, Opinions, and Questions

A significant number of pro-choice people in the church maintain their beliefs because of how they have positioned abortion from a systematic theology framework of absolutes, convictions, opinions, and questions. Systematic theology seeks to answer the question of what the Bible teaches about an issue today. Indeed, we have different denominations, different traditions around baptism or the Lord's Supper, or different doctrinal statements. But some core absolute beliefs must be in place in order to remain true to the Christian faith. For example, whether your church uses grape juice or wine for communion is not as vital to the Christian faith as whether you believe Jesus is the Son of God who died and was raised again after three days.

There are four categories for issues that are debated or debatable within the church.

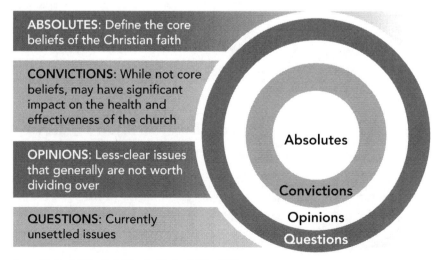

ABSOLUTES: Define the core beliefs of the Christian faith

CONVICTIONS: While not core beliefs, may have significant impact on the health and effectiveness of the church

OPINIONS: Less-clear issues that generally are not worth dividing over

QUESTIONS: Currently unsettled issues

Absolutes
Convictions
Opinions
Questions

Source: The Study Bible, *English Standard Version*, 2008, p. 2507

While the absolutes cannot be compromised, we give some grace for differences in convictions, opinions, and questions. The challenge with beliefs about abortion is the issue gets relegated to opinions or questions, instead of where it should be held—in the absolutes.

Now I know you may be thinking, Roland, how can you say that abortion is on equal footing with Jesus's death and resurrection? Isn't abortion more like the issue of birth control, where some churches, like the Catholic church, have taken a hard stance against it while others have embraced it?

My answer to you is simple: being pro abundant life is as fundamental to our faith as the Great Commission and the Great Commandment. Allowing this "exemption" to loving your neighbor or sacrificing your own desires for another violates these essential Christian principles. Our views around life must be linked and locked on the immutable word of God. Advocating for life can't be a political opinion or even an unsettled church question. We must see issues of life in the ring of absolutes.

If an issue is clearly an absolute and some in the church recategorize it as an opinion or question, there will be disunity. All the way back in the garden of Eden, Adam and Eve were given a clear absolute: do not eat the fruit. But what did Satan do? He questioned Eve. "Did God actually say, 'You shall not eat of any tree in the garden'?…You will not surely die." He turned an absolute into a question and sin ensued.

This is the same thing happening in the church today on many social issues, including abortion. It's an absolute that God is the creator of life and we are created in the image of God, knitted together in our mothers' wombs. It's an absolute that it is a sin to kill innocent life. Evil and injustice always thrive when God's absolutes become our opinions or our questions. So, what must the church do? Let's take a look.

CHAPTER EIGHT

WHAT SHOULD THE CHURCH DO?

A couple of years ago, I had the privilege of speaking at a pastor's event in Texas. The organizer invited me to talk about Care Net and how pastors could help their congregations respond to the abortion issue. I started my presentation with a question: "How many of you became pastors because you wanted to overturn *Roe v. Wade*?"

No one raised their hand.

"How many of you became pastors because you wanted to end abortion in your lifetime?" Still, no hands. So, I asked one last question.

"How many of you became pastors because you felt called to preach the gospel and make disciples of Jesus Christ?"

Every pastor's hand shot up. Discipleship. That's what got these pastors excited. It's the great mission of every God-honoring pastor and any vibrant church because it is the Great Commission of Jesus Christ.

The New Testament tells us that Christ chose for Himself twelve disciples. He poured His life and teaching into these men and, with them, performed His ministry. Though He did not need their help, He chose to minister through them. Isn't that incredible? Christ wanted these men to be an integral part of His work.

THE ALTERNATIVE TO ABORTION

Discipleship was so important to Christ that His last words before returning to heaven were a call to make disciples. In Matthew 28:19–20 (NIV) he said:

> Therefore go and make disciples of all nations, baptizing them in the name of the Father and of the Son and of the Holy Spirit, and teaching them to obey everything I have commanded you. And surely I am with you always, to the very end of the age.

So, they did. Each of His initial disciples (except for Judas) made disciples, who in turn made disciples, who also made disciples, and the gospel of Christ transformed the world.

Likewise, if we want churches to do the "good work" of making abortion unthinkable in their congregations and communities, abortion must be viewed primarily as a discipleship issue. What can the church do to make abortion unthinkable? It can do what it is designed to do best. Make disciples.

How Discipleship Must Shape How We Serve

The most common objection to viewing abortion as a discipleship issue is that our focus should be on meeting the immediate needs of women and men facing abortion decisions. Some say if we get distracted by presenting the gospel or evangelism, we risk alienating those in need of help. They feel it is more important to give whatever material support is needed to choose life and worry about discipleship another time. But when this happens, we leave those considering abortion exactly where we found them spiritually. There is no life change or spiritual transformation to keep them from going down the exact same road again.

This doesn't mean that meeting physical needs is unimportant. If we have the means to help a brother in need and don't, James says that our faith is dead (James 2:14–17). We can't minister to the spiritual needs of our neighbors without also ministering to their physical needs, but we can meet their physical needs without ever touching their spiritual needs.

However, if we really want to see an end to abortion or make abortion unthinkable in this generation, then we must see clients transformed so they don't just choose life (*bios*) for their unborn children, but they also choose abundant life (*zoe*) for their families. This can't happen if we're only meeting their physical and material needs, and this can't happen outside the church's call to make disciples for Jesus Christ. There is only one entity in this nation ideologically aligned to transform lives and structurally capable of dealing with a post-*Roe* environment in a God-honoring way. It is the church. Pregnancy centers do amazing, God-honoring work and are ideologically and theologically aligned to save lives, but the support of pregnancy centers does not extend much beyond birth.

The Guttmacher Institute says about half of all abortions are performed on women who have had a prior abortion.[1] Planned Parenthood's sign on the door says, "Thank you, come again!"

At Care Net affiliated pregnancy centers our doors can't have this sign. We don't want those at risk for abortion to make the same choices that lead back to the same problems. Nor do we want to see their children in the same circumstances as well. Remember the 18/18 Rule?

We have robust governmental and nonprofit social services networks in this nation. These providers may be structurally capable, but the services they provide tend to be transactional. If a struggling woman has two kids out of wedlock and then gets pregnant with a third, these social service providers typically don't challenge her to reconsider how she is living. That's why so many government and social services programs have repeat clients for generations.

If we don't think about this issue in a pro abundant life way, then we become transactional too. A woman comes with one baby and you help her save that one. But then she comes back again. You help her save the second one. She may come back with a third or even a fourth. This is Planned Parenthood's goal, but should not be the goal of any Christian who advocates for life. There's no retail, "repeat customers" with Jesus. He didn't say, come as you are and stay as you were. We don't want people to "come again." If they do return, we want them to return not to be served, but to serve others.

Let's use a hamburger chain as an example. As a retail establishment, its goal is to make repeat customers. They say, "Buy our burgers. Eat more burgers." This retail model is transactional. Success is counted in the number of hamburgers sold. But this is not what Jesus taught.

In pregnancy centers and for everyone working to help men and women make life decisions, we can't view our interactions as transactions. We can't celebrate complete victory when a baby is saved in the same way Chick-fil-A might celebrate a milestone number of chicken sandwiches sold. Yes, we celebrate babies saved. But our aspiration is not that the woman would come back to our centers a second and third time to save more of her babies. Our goal must be that her life is so *transformed* by the gospel of Jesus Christ that we never see her again in this context.

The church's call, modeled after Jesus's ministry, is for all to come as they are but not to stay as they came. Rather they should be transformed by the renewal of their minds. Remember, Jesus only met the vulnerable and socially isolated woman at the well once. He was not transactional, and He did not give her what she thought she needed, physical water *(bios)*. Instead, He told her to call the husband He knew she did not have. Jesus lovingly challenged her to consider how she was living. He gave her spiritual living water *(zoe)* to transform her physically, emotionally, and spiritually. He also reconnected her socially.

To be clear, one cannot be a disciple maker without providing material support. First John 3:17 says, "But if anyone has the world's goods and sees his brother in need, yet closes his heart against him, how does God's love abide in him?" In other words, you can perform social services without making disciples, but you cannot make disciples without providing for material needs.

Our view of political advocacy can be informed in the same way. The government is on God's shoulders (Isaiah 9:6). God uses government to organize the affairs of men (Romans 13:1–7). But what do we know about governments? They can be unjust and unmerciful to the vulnerable. As Christians, we are called to hold our government accountable to be just and merciful. We're called to vote in such a way that holds our government accountable for righteousness and justice.

Again, you can be involved in the political process and not make disciples. But you can't be a disciple maker without being politically involved. Jesus had people coming to Him with all kinds of needs. Some had too many demons, some had too much money, some had too much pride, some had too many husbands. When each of them came to Jesus with those needs, He met them at their point of need *(bios)*. Then what did He do? He called them into discipleship *(zoe)*.

When we view our work through the lens of discipleship, we no longer create repeat customers because we are leading men and women to transformed lives that change their perspective on the whole issue. Our goal should be to help these men and women learn a different way, follow a different path than the one that led them to pregnancy centers or abortion clinics with an unplanned pregnancy. The church is uniquely equipped to fill this role.

Disciples Not Converts

Evangelism is at the heart of Care Net's affiliated pregnancy centers. Clients hear the gospel of Jesus Christ. They get the Good News. Since 2008, Care Net affiliated pregnancy centers have made over two million gospel presentations, which is one reason I'm so blessed to co-labor with thousands of Christ followers to do this God-honoring ministry work.

When sharing the gospel with women in pregnancy centers, we must be careful that we don't end up making converts instead of disciples. Here's how that happens. A woman comes to the pregnancy center. She has that conversion experience after the gospel is presented. She says, "Yes, I want to be a follower of Christ." Then we send her back to the culture. We have missed the important step of connecting her with a community within a church.

Truth is, culture makes disciples too. That's the reason why she's at the pregnancy center. She's facing an unplanned pregnancy because she has become a great disciple of the culture that disconnects God's design for motherhood, fatherhood, sex, and marriage. This unplanned pregnancy is a consequence of walking in the fullness of the culture's teaching.

So, if they come into our affiliated pregnancy centers and we introduce them to Christ, but then send them back to the culture, what do you think the culture will do? I can promise you one thing: it won't teach them Jesus's way. The culture, as a disciple-making entity, requires conformity to its principles and values.

However, the church is the place designed for ongoing discipleship; it is the seat of discipleship. We need the church to fill this role. Pregnancy centers are not designed or called to provide long-term discipleship. Remember, the Great Commission says to teach them all that Christ taught. The pregnancy center can be an evangelical "pre-discipleship" gateway to introduce men and women who have not heard the good news to the transformational power of the gospel. But then we've got to get them connected to our churches for ongoing support and discipleship.

Orphans and Widows

When you hear about a woman facing an abortion decision, is your first thought who you need to vote for so she can't have an abortion? Or do you wonder what kind of material support she needs? Don't get me wrong, these are important considerations. As Christians, I suggest our first thought should be that she needs to be a disciple of Jesus Christ. The baby growing in her womb needs to be a disciple of Jesus Christ, and so does the man who got her pregnant. When we think about the life issue this way, we realize our work does not end when we pull the lever in the voting booth or when we drop off diapers at a pregnancy center.

As Christians, I suggest our first thought should be that she needs to be a disciple of Jesus Christ.

Do you think about the vital role the church must play for every man and woman facing an unplanned pregnancy in meeting their greatest need: their need for Jesus? This is why I no longer call myself just pro-life. This is what it means to be pro abundant life.

Making disciples as we support men and women facing pregnancy decisions is work that integrates into who we are called to be as Christians. James 1:27 says, "Religion that is pure and undefiled before God the Father is this: to visit orphans and widows in their affliction and to keep oneself unstained from the world."

We are to support orphans and widows in their distress, and we are to keep ourselves from being polluted by the world. At the time this was written, an orphan was a child without a father. A widow was often a woman who was already a mother but who was without a husband. All through scripture, you see the measure of righteousness in what you do to care for orphans and widows.

Today there's a nuanced difference. Instead of that husband and father being physically dead, no longer able to fulfill his responsibilities, today's absent husband and father says to the mother and child, "You're dead to me," thereby creating cultural orphans and widows.

As Christ followers, we should care for those cultural orphans and widows—single mothers and their kids. But we also have an opportunity to help bring that father and husband back to life. He doesn't have to stay in the position where he's saying that his woman and child are dead to him. There's a Lazarus moment that needs to happen. A stone needs to be rolled back. And, like Christ, we must call to this man to arise. That's the power we have through Christ, through discipleship. This is a tremendous opportunity for us to restore God's vision for the family.

The Pro Abundant Life Mission and the Church

This is what's so radical and powerful about the pro abundant life mission. Our commitment to saving the lives of the unborn is amplified when we view it through the lens of both the Great Commission and the Great Commandment. Beyond this, we don't just aim to save babies, we do what Christ asks and we share the gospel to save souls. Life decisions need the life support that the church is uniquely positioned and called to provide.

MINISTRY MOMENT   Q CARE●NET.

MAKING LIFE DISCIPLES™

Care Net created the first ever church curriculum designed to engage abortion-vulnerable women and men with the message of abundant life. Making Life Disciples™ (MLD) gives churches tools to enable congregations to offer compassion, hope, help, and discipleship to those who need it most. It also equips churches to build lifesaving partnerships with their local pregnancy centers. Offering ongoing discipleship means clients are less likely to return with another unplanned pregnancy. MLD also enables churches to have an intentional and proactive ministry for those inside the church at risk for abortion.

Care Net's model of service is centered on the belief that the local church is intentionally and strategically designed by God as the only institution ideologically aligned and structurally capable of providing discipleship and long-term care. This is why we believe so strongly in building entry points from the pregnancy center to the local church. Together, we will elevate the assignment for every believer to live out our call to the Great Commission and the Great Commandment.

As Christians we are called to do "good works." Women inside and outside the church in these situations crave the compassion, hope, and help found in people who live out Christ's call to love their neighbors as themselves. This is why Christ told His disciples that they would be known by their love (John 13:35). But all the good works that Christians do must connect to our greater mission: making disciples. We do good works for the same reason that Jesus did good works, which was to make disciples.

In other areas of life, it's easy to see how our works must be anchored in the Great Commission. As the Church supplies water for the thirsty, food for the hungry, clothes for the naked, compassion for the orphan, and homes for the homeless, Christians intuitively understand they can support these organizations. Yet, many of us choose to support Christian ministries rather than secular organizations doing these works because we also want the gospel to be shared. We want to invest in kingdom work that links *bios* to *zoe*. But is that how you think about the life issue?

If we think about it primarily through the lens of discipleship, then abortion is no longer an issue that you think about once every four years during election season, or once a year on Sanctity of Life Sunday. Every day becomes Sanctity of Life Day because we're called to make disciples every day. So, I ask you, is this how you think about abortion?

Render to Caesar

There's a story in scripture where Jesus was given a coin. He was asked by one of the Pharisees about paying taxes. Rome used the profits of taxation to enact unjust and immoral policies. So, from that perspective, the Pharisee wondered, was it lawful as a God-fearing Jew to pay for such policies? It was a trick question designed to trap Jesus. If He said no, they'd say He was encouraging insurrection. If He said yes, they'd say He was in support of an immoral government.

Jesus did neither. Instead, He asked them for a coin. "Whose likeness and inscription is this?" He asked. "Caesar's" they replied. So, Christ said, "Therefore render to Caesar the things that are Caesar's, and to God the things that are God's" (Matthew 22:20–21).

His point could not have been clearer. Money and commerce bore the image of Caesar because they belonged to his realm. Caesar was primarily concerned about the material and physical. Men and women, however, bear the image of God. The coin may belong to Caesar, but we belong to our creator. Christ's command was to pay taxes and redeem souls; to feed the hungry their daily bread and to give the hungry the bread of life. Christ called us to bring all creation back under submission to God, not just smooth over society's rough edges.

Ministering to those considering abortion is no different. If all we do is reach out and meet their physical needs, we won't accomplish what Christ commanded. We will operate only in Caesar's realm instead of God's. Caesar didn't care about eternity in a Christian sense; transformation wasn't on Caesar's radar. It was all transactional to Caesar.

In contrast, Jesus always cares about transformation. When the woman caught in adultery was thrown at His feet, Jesus met her physical need for protection by ensuring she wouldn't be stoned. He then addressed her spiritual need of transformation by forgiving her sin and calling her to "go and sin no more." He didn't leave her where He found her. Indeed, Christ's call is always to come as you are but not to stay as you came.

CHAPTER NINE

ARE YOU PRO ABUNDANT LIFE?

Given the title of this book, it won't surprise you that I wrote it with a very specific intention—to encourage you to become pro abundant life. In chapter two, I introduced the graphic below to illustrate the pro abundant life framework as a structure with the roof supported by two pillars.

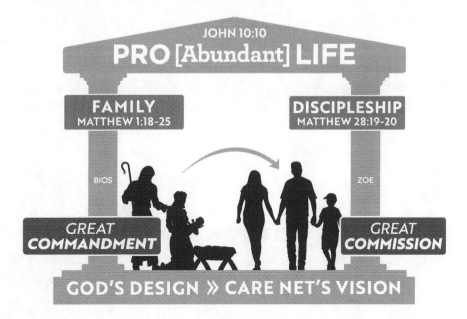

To review, the roof is Jesus's "why" statement from John 10:10, where Jesus states that He came that we may have life and have life abundantly. So, Jesus was pro abundant life. But how do we get this abundant life? God provided two distinct and divine covenant-building entities, which I've designated as pillars, to make this possible. The first pillar is God's design for family. In the nativity narrative of the birth of Christ we discussed in the previous chapters, when Mary was faced with an unplanned pregnancy from a human perspective, God created a family. Consequently, Mary's unplanned pregnancy did not become a crisis pregnancy.

This manger family is a model for the modern family as God designed it. When a woman embraces the inspiration and character of Mary and the man who got her pregnant is inspired to take action like Joseph, the woman is less likely to have an abortion. She gives her baby in the womb physical life *(bios)* outside the womb.

But as John 10:10 clearly states, Christ wants people inside and outside the womb to have heartbeats that are heaven bound. He came that we might have eternal life *(zoe)* too. And this leads to the second pillar—God's call to discipleship. Therefore, as pro abundant life people, we must work just as Christ did to connect people to the church for ongoing support and discipleship.

There is one last key aspect that I would like to point out. You will note the family pillar has the words "Great Commandment," and the discipleship pillar has the words "Great Commission." I added these words to the pillars so you can truly see how connected the life issue is to the call and mission of every Christian and to the church. Specifically, God created the family, and the role of the family is to live out the sacrificial love of the Great Commandment and to model this framework for the broader society. In fact, every conflict in the family and in society at large happens because there is a failure to love God, love your neighbor, or love yourself. Remember, the Great Commandment was present in the garden of Eden with Adam and Eve, the first family.

The second pillar, discipleship, is the role of the church as it fulfills the Great Commission to make disciples of all nations. This discipleship process is to be modeled first in the family and then in the neighborhood and broader community. This is God's design and why it's essential to be pro abundant life. When you're pro abundant life, you are focused on God's design for family and God's call to discipleship. You are living out the Great Commandment to fulfill the Great Commission.

So, are you pro abundant life?

Turning Your Pro Abundant Life Passion into Action

As I observe the nearly fifty years of the pro-life movement, I see many things worth celebrating. I see lives that have been saved, thousands of pregnancy centers working in communities, and some churches mobilized to meet the needs of clients. I have heard countless stories of lives forgiven and set free after they received healing from past abortions. These are all great victories.

However, I also know that as many as 2,800 unborn babies will lose their lives in abortions today and another 2,800 tomorrow. Within forty-eight hours of you reading this sentence, abortion will have taken more lives than the terrorists on September 11. These unborn children need not just laws to protect them, but also men and women whose hearts have been transformed by the gospel who are ready to disciple any woman and man considering abortion.

For too long we have disproportionately attacked abortion primarily with the tools of Caesar. Our focus has been on reforming the legal climate and meeting material needs, but we haven't aggressively focused on the spiritual rot at the heart of our culture. Ephesians 6:12 reminds us that our battle is not primarily against flesh and blood, but rather against spiritual forces of evil in the heavenly realm. Indeed, Christ shows us a better way.

One day, Christ took His disciples to Mount Hermon, the site locals believed contained a passage into hell. Pagan worshippers would feast, drink, and engage in debauched revelry at its base. God-fearing Jews would not venture near such rampant immorality, yet this is precisely where Jesus led His disciples. Faced with such evil, Christ promised that He would build His church and the gates of hell would not prevail against it (Matthew

16:18). He wanted His disciples to know that all the evil of that mountain and all the immoral behavior it came to represent could not resist the power of His church.

Gates are not offensive structures. They are defensive and they don't move. Christ's clear implication was that His disciples were to be engaged in offensive combat, to literally tear down the gates of hell, brick by brick.

Abortion is a "Mount Hermon" not only in our culture and politics, but also in too many churches. This proverbial gate of hell must be torn down. We need to ask ourselves if we, as a pro abundant life movement, are attacking this gate the way God said we should.

Notice God did not say the state would defeat hell. It was His church. Yet there has been a perspective that this is the pro-life movement's work and the church is helping. But it is exactly the opposite. This is the church's work and the pro-life movement is here to help. Care Net and its affiliated pregnancy centers are parachurch ministries. *Para* means to come alongside the church. A lawyer has a paralegal on staff to complete a specific task for the client. However, the client relationship belongs to the lawyer, not the paralegal. So it is with pregnancy center ministries that come alongside the church. Clients who come to pregnancy centers are members of churches that just don't know it yet! When you view the abortion issue through a pro abundant life perspective, this is crystal clear: the church must lead. And pastors, as the uniquely called and faithful shepherds of the church, must lead the way.

How does the church defeat the gates of hell? By living out the Great Commandment to fulfill the Great Commission.

Ensuring Heartbeats are Heaven Bound

If you've ever taken an emergency training class, you may remember one of the first steps before CPR or checking vital signs is to identify someone to call 911. You're taught not to just yell to the crowd, "Someone call 911," but instead to assign someone specific to the task. "You in the green shirt! You call 911!" This is important because unless someone is assigned the task, it's unclear who should do it. It's ironic that in emergency situations, if something is everyone's responsibility, it's no one's responsibility.

Church, we have an emergency situation here, and I'm asking you to respond to the 911 call. By church, I mean you and me. As followers of Jesus, we are his church and it's not an overstatement to say that lives are in the balance. You have a role. I have a role. We all have a role in saving lives. This is the very essence of the Great Commandment and the Great Commission. You go. You do. And while we may not be called upon when someone's having a heart attack, we have a tremendous opportunity to save the beating hearts of babies who would otherwise face abortion. Who will respond if you don't? If it's everybody's responsibility to call 911, no one calls. Will you do it? Are you inspired? Well, inspiration is like perspiration. It dries up if there is no action. So, I ask you, will you take your passion for the unborn and put it into action?

Care Net's Comprehensive Gospel-Focused Strategy

I had no idea how to prevent abortion within the church. This really convicted me to do more in my local church to advocate for life. I think Care Net's approach to the pro-life movement is the best way to go about it—in a loving, compassionate, Christlike way. It makes me excited to be part of a movement that is considerate and effectively tackling this overwhelming challenge.

— *Miranda, Volunteer at a Care Net affiliate*

Recently, I watched a documentary about the planning of D-day. Hitler and the Nazis had taken much territory and it looked as though there was no stopping the forces of evil that Hitler's regime represented. But a plan was developed that turned the tables—a massive invasion on the beaches of Normandy, France.

However, there was a big problem. The Nazis had built a substantial fortification of deadly guns strategically positioned to thwart any invasion. These fortifications were protected by the formidable German air force. Therefore, the allies determined that they had to get air superiority before they could take back the territory the Nazis had gained and defeat them once and for all. And that's exactly what they did.

Care Net has a multitude of strategic gospel-centered initiatives to end abortion. But there's one initiative that has unlimited power to change hearts, minds, and lives—prayer. We are reminded that our ultimate battle is not against the "flesh and blood" of the abortion provider and those who support them. It's against the spiritual forces of evil in the heavenly realm. To regain the ground the forces of evil have captured in our homes, churches, and culture, we must gain air superiority with steadfast prayer. So, a central aspect of Care Net's approach is its Abundant Life Prayer Network.

Just like in the battle on D-day, we need to have troops on the ground. But if we want to win, it's essential to have air support from prayer warriors who cover vulnerable babies in the womb, women and men at risk for abortion, churches and pastors, our affiliated pregnancy centers, volunteers, leaders, and legislators in prayer. This "prayer force" destroys the strongholds that make abortion possible so ground troops can have victory. *Amen!* Consequently, one of the first things that I would encourage you to do to turn your pro abundant life passion into action is go to www.makinglifedisciples.com/pray-with-us to join this national prayer initiative or use the below QR code.

Care Net's Lifesaving Strategies

Care Net has developed Four Key Strategies designed to serve the unique needs of women and men at risk for abortion. Each strategy encourages choosing life for unborn children and mobilization of the culture—especially the church—to make abortion unthinkable.

ABUNDANT LIFE PRAYER NETWORK

PRAYER

proud affiliate CARE NET

CARE NET U

Pregnancy Centers are local, nonprofit ministries that provide compassionate support to women and men faced with difficult pregnancy decisions. Care Net provides centers with the training and resources they need to serve their local communities with excellence.

making LIFE DISCIPLES

ABORTION RECOVERY & CARE · ARC ·

Care Net is equipping churches to offer compassion, hope, help, and discipleship to women and men in their communities that are facing pregnancy decisions. Care Net also offers spiritual and emotional post-abortion recovery and care resources.

CARE NET

4 KEY STRATEGIC INITIATIVES

1 EMERGENCY CARE

2 SHORT-TERM CARE

3 LONG-TERM CARE

4 INFLUENCING the CULTURE

Building Bridges

Stopping the Cycle

pregnancy DECISION LINE

Pregnancy Decision Line (PDL) is Care Net's strategic initiative that provides immediate pregnancy decision coaching to women and men at risk for abortion. PDL coaches also offer the hope of the Gospel and connect callers to local affiliated pregnancy centers to further support a life decision.

PRO [Abundant] LIFE

Care Net seeks to influence the culture by transforming hearts and minds so that regardless of what the laws are, abortion becomes unthinkable in our homes, churches, and communities. Care Net's goal is to turn pro ABUNDANT life passion into action.

ABUNDANT LIFE PRAYER NETWORK

PRAYER

A person who has a heart attack needs a continuum of care. He'll start with emergency care from the paramedics triggered by the initial 911 call. This is a time-sensitive, on-the-spot intervention in a crisis. An ambulance transports the patient to short-term care at the hospital to stabilize him. To prevent another emergency event, he's connected to a long-term primary care physician to address the underlying issues related to the way he's living that triggered the heart attack in the first place. The goal is to never see this guy in the same crisis again.

Care Net's first three strategic initiatives offer similar categories of ministry care. The difference is that Care Net is not just focused on the physical aspects of care (*bios*), but also the spiritual aspects (*zoe*). Our emergency care is our Pregnancy Decision Line (PDL)—staffed by trained and experienced nurses and nonmedical coaches. From the initial call to PDL, we seek to have a gospel-focused interaction that leads to making a disciple for Jesus Christ.

This team fields calls from women and men all over the country facing emergency situations—people determined to have abortions. The goal of PDL is to connect clients to pregnancy centers across the country. The short-term care offered by these fantastic pregnancy centers meets clients at their point of need from conception to birth by offering practical resources, parenting education, and other support.

Finally, the goal of this short-term care approach is to transition clients from the pregnancy center to the church for ongoing support and discipleship as soon as possible. That's the idea behind Making Life Disciples (MLD), which equips churches to care for those facing pregnancy decisions and to disciple women and men most at risk for abortion. We also need to minister to those with past abortions through Abortion Recovery and Care (ARC). These hurting folks need to be forgiven and set free to reach those who may want to make the same mistake.

In the next section, I'll explain more about each of these ministry programs. The important thing to notice is that each plays a critical role. If we don't offer emergency care through PDL, those facing a crisis may turn to abortion providers for advice and never hear the truth that their baby's life is worth saving. The pregnancy centers are vital to our strategy, but unless we equip and train the church to play a role in teaching Christians how to be pro abundant life, we may create repeat customers for our affiliated centers. Finally, for those who have already had an abortion, it's vital that Care Net has a way to rehabilitate, restore, and reconnect women and men to the Savior who can heal any guilt or shame. Just like with a recovering heart patient, if we don't do long-term care right, women and men will face another emergency situation.

Emergency Care: Care Net's Pregnancy Decision Line

The Pregnancy Decision Line (PDL) was launched in 2012 as a result of the experience of Melinda Delahoyde, Care Net's then-president. Care Net partnered with another ministry to run a call center that referred women at risk for abortion to pregnancy centers. Melinda listened to a harrowing call with a woman who needed immediate help and pregnancy decision coaching. She was crying, desperate, and potentially suicidal as a result of the news of her pregnancy. However, all the call handler was trained to do was refer her to a pregnancy center. But that presented a huge problem because the pregnancy center was closed.

Haunted by this caller's desperation, Melinda wanted to create a unique call center that would provide real-time pregnancy decision coaching for women like this caller and for women and men who may be reluctant to visit a pregnancy center. Thus, PDL was born.

In God's providence, the post-*Roe* environment requires PDL's unique ministry model now more than ever. An alarming 63 percent of abortions now occur via the abortion pill. As a result, every bathroom in every home or college dorm room is now a potential abortion clinic. Prior to the ubiquity of the abortion pill, which is readily available online or at many local pharmacies, it was generally nine days from the time a woman confirmed her pregnancy until she scheduled her abortion.

As a result, every bathroom in every home or college dorm room is now a potential abortion clinic.

Unfortunately, now the timeline has gone from nine days to nine inches—the distance from her hand to her mouth with the abortion pill. Many PDL callers have their abortion pills when they make the call.

The real-time ministry aspect of PDL is essential. PDL coaches frequently get calls from women who regret their abortions. These women can be quickly connected to Care Net's Abortion Recovery and Care (ARC) ministry for healing and restoration. Some are traumatized by seeing the fetal remains of the abortion. I recall one especially difficult situation where the father of the woman who had aborted her baby called PDL because his daughter was distraught after seeing her aborted baby. His wife went to his daughter's home and was on her way back home with their grandchild in a plastic bag, and he wasn't sure what they should do with it.

Consider the story of Layla, one common to so many of our PDL callers. Layla didn't believe she was ready to have a baby. A friend knew of a pharmacy that didn't require a prescription for abortion pills, so it seemed to be Layla's best option. Scared and not knowing what to do, she followed the abortion pill procedure at ten weeks. Feeling like maybe it hadn't worked, she called PDL. The coach encouraged her to go to the emergency room for an ultrasound, which determined the baby was still alive. Though Layla was worried her baby may have birth defects, the obstetrician told her the baby looked fine. Seeing the ultrasound convinced Layla that the baby was a life worth saving. Our coach followed up with her the next day, and Layla decided to carry the baby to term and become a mother.

PDL is a critical emergency care first responder on the front lines of the abortion issue. That's why PDL coaches always seek to initiate spiritual conversations with callers right from the start. They pray with clients on the initial and follow up calls and ask questions like, "Do you have a spiritual understanding or faith that is informing your decision to abort?" It is never too soon to engage the transforming power of Christ. Remember, all of Care Net's ministry initiatives are guided by a pro abundant life perspective in word and ministry deed. PDL, like all Care Net initiatives, is focused on making disciples for Jesus Christ amid the most difficult situations.

Support of PDL is now more important than ever because there has been a proposal to set up a federal "decision line" of sorts. Under Title X funding (which has become a key funding source for abortion providers), a national hotline may soon be created to refer women to pregnancy-related health services, including abortion.

For this reason, Care Net is continuously evaluating and expanding the services we offer through PDL. For example, we now have nurses who can answer questions about the abortion pill and other abortion procedures that require more medical expertise. We've also updated our website, pregnancydecisionline.org, to include more resources, information, testimonials, referrals, and information on state abortion laws, as well as made it easier for women and men to find local pregnancy centers. Because connecting women and men to someone who cares is vital to our support model, we make "warm transfers" to local pregnancy centers. While the caller is still on the call with PDL, we seek to set the pregnancy center appointment in real time.

Pro Abundant Life in Action: Ways You Can Get Involved

- **Visit PDL website (pregnancydecisionline.org)**: This site provides an understanding of the critical ministry support that is offered.

- **Post PDL information in your church**: This is especially important because someone facing a pregnancy decision, especially in your church, needs an immediate lifeline. Having PDL's website (pregnancydecisionline.org) and phone number (866-799-8021) posted on bulletin boards and in restrooms is critical.

- **Pray for the PDL ministry team**: Engaging someone via phone or text who is determined to abort their baby is extremely difficult. PDL coaches need an abundance of prayer. I encourage you to pray Ephesians 6:11–20 that they may be protected by and equipped with the full armor of God as they battle the spiritual forces of evil that abortion represents.

- **Sponsor a PDL Day**: Many Care Net ministry partners have committed to fund a day of PDL. This is a fantastic way to support this vital ministry outreach. You can visit care-net.org/PDL to learn more.

Short-Term Care: The Critically Important Role of Pregnancy Centers

Supporting pregnancy centers is Care Net's first and oldest ministry initiative. This important work started shortly after *Roe v. Wade* became law. As abortion providers rushed to establish clinics across the nation, committed and compassionate Christians responded by establishing life-affirming pregnancy centers.

Over time, it was clear to the growing number of local pregnancy centers that additional support was needed. So, they approached a ministry called Christian Action Council, which was founded by theologians Francis Schaeffer and Harold O. J. Brown, and former US Surgeon General C. Everett Koop, with counsel from Reverend Billy Graham, for training, resources, and technical assistance. As the demands for support grew, the Christian Action Council started a project called the Care Network to meet the need. Eventually, the Christian Action Council made the strategic decision to focus all its efforts on its growing network of affiliated pregnancy centers and changed its name to Care Net.

Today, Care Net has an affiliated network of over 1,200 pregnancy centers in the US and Canada. Since 2008, this network of pregnancy centers has saved more than 1,081,210 lives from abortion and made over 2,124,931 gospel presentations. Care Net affiliated pregnancy centers save local communities over 96 million dollars annually by providing material support to women and men at risk for abortion.

It is a blessing to support these truly amazing women and men who have dedicated their lives to offer compassion, hope, and help to women and men faced with pregnancy decisions; to help them choose life for their unborn babies and abundant life for their families. These dedicated folks provide steadfast encouragement to pregnancy center clients to support life-affirming options like parenting and adoption.

To facilitate this critical support for affiliates, Care Net provides access to high-quality resources as well as online and in-person training. This support is not only available for pregnancy center staff, but also for board members and more than 30,000 volunteers who support local pregnancy centers. In addition,

Care Net hosts an annual national conference where nearly 1,300 of its affiliated pregnancy center staff gather for training, encouragement, and fellowship.

Care Net affiliated pregnancy centers and their volunteers are changing lives. Here's one story of how this kind of life change is happening.

It's really easy to get an abortion in Washington, DC, which means people from other states actually travel there to get abortions. On one cold winter day, a pregnancy center volunteer named Julia stood on the sidewalk outside a DC abortion clinic. Julia didn't let the frigid temps stop her from ministering that day, though. She started a light-hearted conversation about the temperature with a woman named Isabel, whom Julia soon discovered had traveled from New Jersey to get an abortion that day. In fact, Julia found out that the abortion clinic had actually paid the woman's travel expenses to come to the clinic and had paid to put her up in a hotel. Right before Isabel entered the clinic, Julia gently whispered, "Hey, I just wanted you to know there are other options. I would be willing to walk with you to think through other options." Isabel shrugged and responded, "Thanks," but then went into the clinic. While sitting in the waiting room, Isabel started thinking more about the conversation she'd just had with Julia. Isabel got up from her chair and told the receptionist, "I'm not going to do this today," and walked back out. She made a beeline to Julia, who was still standing there in the bitter cold, and said, "Will you help me?" Julia and another volunteer got in the car with Isabel and drove her back to New Jersey, where they helped her get connected with a pregnancy care center and a church. By the grace of God, Isabel chose to have her baby.

When I think about the lifesaving work of Care Net affiliates, I'm reminded of the story of the woman at the well that I referenced in chapter four. She is an archetype for every woman that ever comes to a pregnancy center. Jesus's request for her to "call her husband" is the impetus for Care Net to make reaching the father of the baby an essential aspect of Care Net's ministry approach. From a pro abundant life perspective, we seek to promote

God's design for the family, which includes the father. However, our goal is not just for this man to become an unmarried "baby daddy," but as much as possible a Joseph-minded husband and father.

It has truly been a blessing to see how this aspect of Care Net's ministry has flourished. When I joined Care Net in 2012, a very small percentage of affiliates had any form of outreach or support for the father of the baby. Now, nearly 70 percent of affiliated pregnancy centers do, with many having men on-site to work with the father as the mother is receiving care. To accelerate the growth in this ministry area, in 2022 Care Net hosted the first ever pro-life men's conference, Called and Missioned. Care Net also launched two comprehensive fatherhood projects with selected affiliated centers to codify best practices and refined resources like Doctor Dad®, our signature training for new and expectant fathers. Doctor Dad's focus is to help the father of the baby develop skills to enable him to be a full partner in raising his new baby. His enhanced parenting skills increase the mother's confidence that she will have the support needed, which reduces the likelihood of an abortion. One of our volunteers shared a story of what happened when he introduced a new client to the program.

When I suggested that Billy (a client with multi-agency involvement) take Doctor Dad and explained the format, he jumped at the chance, shooting the QR code in my office. Billy was consistent in his course activity, and speaking to him regularly, he continuously expressed how he was affected by Doctor Dad. Our discussions often led to thoughts about his own dad and his experiences as a father. When he completed the course, which is incentivized, I asked what gift card he thought he would like to receive. He said he would like to be able to do something nice for his wife. As a result of his efforts, Billy and his wife got to do something that finances had not recently allowed; they went to dinner at one of their favorite restaurants.

— *Matthew, NYC Fatherhood Champion*

Here's another testimony.

> It worked. Praise the Lord and thank you. I had a young man come in fifteen minutes ago who will now be our first Doctor Dad client. I had the sweetest moment with this guy. After I was done sharing about the nuts and bolts of Doctor Dad he asked me, "Why do you do this?" I told him, "Because I care about you and if I don't, who will?" He started to weep. All that to say, it's been a good day!

— *Kirk, Texas Fatherhood Champion*

The short-term care that pregnancy centers provide is critical. But as pro abundant life people focused on *bios* and *zoe,* pregnancy centers must be connected to the church in order for clients to get ongoing support and discipleship. Remember, pregnancy centers can do evangelism—present the gospel—which leads to making converts. But we are not called to make converts. We are called to make disciples. As we discussed in chapter eight, only the church is designed for the long-term ministry task to teach all that Christ taught, to make disciples who make disciples that live and love like Jesus.

All our affiliated pregnancy centers are doing amazing work, and the stories that come from these centers are a steady stream of encouragement and inspiration. It's important to remember that pregnancy centers are generally equipped to help women and men for a year or less. After the baby is born, pregnancy center clients need a place to be connected where they can receive ongoing support, care, and, if they've made a decision or renewed decision for faith, discipleship. This is not the role of the pregnancy center, but of the local church.

Pro Abundant Life in Action: Ways You Can Get Involved

- **Pray for pregnancy center staff:** Like those who minister through PDL, pregnancy center staff need your prayer coverage. Not only is this type of ministry difficult, since the overturning of *Roe v. Wade*, pregnancy center staff have been harassed and threatened with physical violence. Pregnancy centers have also been vandalized and firebombed. Moreover, in many states, pro-choice elected officials are trying to limit, or even stop, their lifesaving services. So your prayer support is very much needed.

- **Volunteer at a local pregnancy center**: Care Net affiliates are always in need of good volunteers to assist in a range of client-supporting activities. There is an especially urgent need for more men to volunteer to minister to the growing number of men who are coming to the pregnancy center with the mother of their unborn child. You can go to pregnancydecisiononline.org to find a pregnancy center close to you.

- **Attend a pregnancy center's annual banquet**: This is one of most meaningful ways to support your local pregnancy center and learn more about their lifesaving work. For many pregnancy centers, this is the biggest fundraising event of the year, so there's a great opportunity to financially support the center.

- **Invite the pregnancy center executive director to speak at your church**: One of the best ways to get the word out about the important work of pregnancy centers is to have someone from the centers speak at your church. This person can speak to the entire congregation as well as the women's and men's ministries. A recent Lifeway survey found only 7 percent of churches have had someone from a pregnancy center speak to the congregation, and seven out of ten churches report having no involvement with pregnancy centers.[1]

Long-Term Care: Church Engagement

The local church plays a vital role in the pro abundant life movement because it is the only organization structurally capable and ideologically aligned to offer long-term support, guidance, and discipleship for women and men who are at risk for abortion or who have made past abortion decisions. Consequently,

Care Net equips churches to offer compassion, hope, help, and discipleship to women and men in their communities in these circumstances in two ways. First, Care Net's Making Life Disciples (MLD) program provides training to help churches become more abundant life minded and to come alongside those facing abortion decisions. Second, Care Net's Abortion Recovery and Care (ARC) programs—Forgiven and Set Free for women and Reclaiming Fatherhood for men—offer healing as well as spiritual and emotional support for women and men who have had abortions.

Pre-Abortion Intervention— Making Life Disciples (MLD)

Many churches have small Bible study groups that meet regularly. But often our small groups are focused on us loving us. What if our small groups were trained and equipped to be about the ministry of us loving them—coming alongside women at risk for abortion at pregnancy centers and in the church to offer compassion, hope, help, and discipleship.

That's how MLD is designed to work. Remember the "Support Needed by Mothers and Children" chart? Recall that a woman is making an abortion decision based on the support she has after birth. The abortion issue is really about nine months and one second. Especially if the father is uninvolved, the key is to get her life support during the conception to birth phase. That's the goal of MLD.

To do this, people in small groups need to be trained for this unique mission field. If one was going on a mission trip to a place they had never been, the church gives cross-cultural training. Most people have never seriously considered killing one of their children or anybody else's. This is a place they've never been. However, a woman and man considering abortion are doing just that. People who seek to minister to these women and men need the unique training that MLD provides to effectively minister to this challenging mission field.

There is tremendous value and potential in this ministry approach. There are only about 3,000 pregnancy centers in the entire United States, but there are nearly 310,000 churches. If just 1 percent of churches implemented this discipleship focus response to abortion, there would be more points of compassion in communities than all the pregnancy centers in the nation. If a pregnancy center could call the MLD coordinator at your church and transition a client who's considering abortion from the pregnancy center to your church for ongoing support and discipleship, it would dramatically reduce the number of abortions. Moreover, if you had a visible ministry like MLD in your church, a Christian woman who wakes up Sunday morning to a positive pregnancy test that she thinks is negative news would never think that Planned Parenthood or other abortion providers are a compassionate alternative to the church. Even if she chooses abortion, as Christians we're called to love her nonetheless because we're called to make disciples. Accordingly, we would be there to give the abortion healing and restoration she needs, just like Jesus was there to help restore the apostle Peter after he "aborted" Jesus and failed to choose the way, the truth, and the life. Here's just one story of how MLD is making a difference.

One of the women in my MLD class sent me a text and she said she needed to talk to me before class. We set up a virtual meeting. With tears streaming down her face she said, "My teenage daughter is seven weeks pregnant." We talked and I supported her and gave her local resources for her daughter. We prayed together and then in our next class she shared the news with our group. God is allowing all of us to walk with this courageous young woman and her mom to experience MLD firsthand. This mom did not know why she was supposed to take the class, she just obeyed God's leading, and now she has an opportunity to save her daughter and grandchild from the trauma of abortion. One person can make a difference and MLD has equipped us to do just that.

— *Toni, MLD participant*

Post-Abortion Intervention—
Abortion Recovery and Care (ARC)

I remember that first night when I sat down at a table with a handful of women I'd never met. Without having to confess, my secret was already out, because we all had the same secret. Walking alongside these women gave me the freedom to open my heart and to stop hiding.

— Angela

Angela, a participant in Forgiven and Set Free, experienced the life change that is possible when women and men are able to heal from the aftermath of abortion in a caring, Christ-centered community. Many women and men who have faced abortion get stuck in the "secret," as Angela called it. The guilt and shame over what they've done keeps them silent in the pews instead of active in work they can understand in a deeper way than most. Care Net's philosophy models that which we see in scripture. Remember how we looked at Peter's abortion of Christ in his three denials of their connection? Oh, what guilt and shame Peter must have felt. Chances are, his denials were his secret. We have no evidence that he told the other disciples what he had done. Why would he?

Scripture tells us that Peter went back to fishing. I'm sure he thought his ministry was over. He'd done the unthinkable and now it was time for him to just stay quiet and go back to what he knew. How could he ever be restored? Hadn't he disqualified himself from ministry?

But Jesus didn't give up on Peter. Instead, Jesus gave Peter what he needed most in the wake of his sin and shame. He needed forgiveness, restoration, and to be given a new mission. Jesus forgave Peter and put him right back into action.

Satan tries to sideline many men and women who've experienced abortion, telling them that their shame and secret are too great for them to ever be effective for Jesus. This is just a lie of the enemy. That's why Care Net developed Abortion Recovery and Care programs for churches to help engage men and women and let them know that they can be forgiven and set free. One participant explained, "I was stuck. He got me good! I was living in a sick mindset believing lies and justifying every abortion. I can breathe again. A weight of heaviness I've lived with so long is gone. I didn't even realize it was there until it wasn't. I leave here renewed, refreshed, and reborn."

Pro Abundant Life in Action: Ways You Can Get Involved

- **Start a Making Life Disciples (MLD) ministry in your church**: A great way to turn your pro abundant life passion into action is to start a MLD ministry, especially as part of your small group ministry outreach. Remember, the goal of MLD is to equip people in the church to offer compassion, hope, help, and discipleship to women and men at risk for abortion. Go to MakingLifeDisciples.com to learn how to get started via online, in a group setting. MLD is also available on RightNow Media.

- **Start an Abortion Recovery and Care ministry in your church**: If you have experienced an abortion, it's important that you receive God's healing and freedom. Please visit AbortionHealing.org to get started on that journey. Given the number of people sitting in pews that have experienced abortion, there's a desperate need to have an abortion healing ministry in every church. I encourage you to be prayerful about starting this important ministry in your church.

- **Facilitate Sanctity of Human Life Sunday in your church**: You can go to MakingLifeDisciples.com to get a free kit that contains all the resources you need to launch this program at your church. This important kit will help you foster a stronger relationship between your church and the local pregnancy center so that Sanctity of Life Sunday becomes sanctity of life every day.

- **Become a Making Life Disciple or Abortion Recovery and Care regional volunteer**: Care Net's goal is to have these ministry platforms available in every church. To do so, we seek to inspire an army of volunteers to reach beyond their home churches to promote these critical ministries. Accordingly, please prayerfully consider if God is calling you to this role. If so, please visit www.MakingLifeDisciples.com/get-connected/.

Influencing the Culture

Care Net is committed to being a compelling and winsome voice of compassion and reason in the public square to challenge the culture to think critically about the value of life, the importance of marriage and strong families, and the transforming power of the gospel of Jesus Christ. Consequently, Care Net reaches about seventeen million people annually through its social media platforms and website. People who engage with Care Net are inspired to sign up for the Abundant Life blog, take free online courses, and download devotionals, research, and e-books. The goal is to help people turn their pro abundant life passion into action on behalf of those at risk for abortion and the unborn children affected by their pregnancy decisions.

Although Care Net's outreach appeals to the broader culture, there is a specific focus on reaching and engaging the church and Christians because Care Net seeks to replicate Christ's ministry approach. When Christ launched His ministry, He could have started with the broader culture, but He didn't. Although the broader culture benefited from His ministry, His focus was initially on reaching the Jewish people—the people of the Book. Spiritual transformation was to start in Jerusalem and then spread to the outer parts of the world. Jesus knew well that if the people of the Book were not seeking righteousness and biblical justice, especially for the most vulnerable, then the rest of the culture would not do so as well. He had to remove the log in their eyes before they would be able to remove the speck in the culture's eyes.

There is a similar dynamic today with the abortion issue. Studies show 54 percent of women who have abortions profess to be Protestant or Catholic. If Jesus were on earth today seeking to address the sin of abortion, where would he focus his attention? Of course, he would start in the church, because if the church and Christians are not seeking righteousness and justice for the most vulnerable in the womb, then the broader culture will never be. As a

Christ-centered ministry, we are following Jesus's example for influencing culture by placing our highest focus on reaching Christians, especially those who profess to be pro-choice. (See Apologetic on page 138, *Is the Pro-Choice Position Consistent with the Life and Teachings of Jesus Christ?*)

Pro Abundant Life in Action:
Ways You Can Get Involved

- **Visit Care Net's website (care-net.org)**: This is a key way to turn your pro abundant life passion into action. At the site, you can join the movement and stay up to date by receiving exclusive updates on the latest pro abundant life news and perspectives from experts at Care Net. You can access free resources like online courses, e-books, devotionals, and research. You can also sign up to receive Care Net's blog, which includes pro abundant life stories, news, and analysis.

- **Follow Care Net on Facebook**: Care Net has an active Facebook presence that keeps followers updated on our lifesaving work. Be sure to share your comments and stories with others in the pro abundant life movement.

- **Give copies of this book to your pastor and others**: Most likely many in your network have not heard the perspective that I shared in this book. It's especially important to reach pastors, since they must lead on the abortion issue. So please help get the word out!

- **Visit the Care Net store**: Click the Store button on Care Net's site to access booklets to share with others. I have written small booklets like *Why We Can't End Abortion Without Discipleship* and *Is the Pro-Choice Position Consistent with The Life and Teachings of Jesus Christ?* that are great conversation starters for your pro-life and pro-choice family members, friends, and colleagues.

- **Consider becoming a Care Net Ministry Partner**: Since the overturn of *Roe v. Wade*, the need for your help is greater than ever. Pro-choice giants continue to push the abortion agenda on women and men facing unexpected pregnancies. I hope you will prayerfully consider becoming a Ministry Partner. Visit care-net.org and click on "Support Care Net" to learn ways to give.

A Final Word: Adopting Jesus's Ministry Model

If we're to love and lead people like Jesus did, it's important for the Church to look at how Jesus ministered to others. In the scriptures, Jesus displayed two distinct ministry models: retrieving and receiving. We see His retrieving model in how He got his first disciples. He saw Peter and Andrew fishing, and He told them to follow Him so He would make them fishers of men (Matthew 4:18).

However, we see His receiving model in His approach with the woman with the issue of blood (Matthew 9:20–22). The woman had been suffering with her condition for twelve years. It's worth noting abortion is an issue of blood—the procedure is bloody, and the baby is the mother and father's flesh and blood. In her desperation, all she could do was crawl in the dirt, the dust, and the dung to grab the tassel of Jesus's robe. And when she did this, not only was she healed physically, but she was also healed emotionally and restored spiritually and socially.

We see both ministry models in action when Jesus is walking on the water and Peter, on the boat, sees Jesus and wants to come to him (Matthew 14:22–33). Jesus told him to come on out, the water was fine. Since this was Peter's idea, like the woman with the issue of blood, Jesus was going to receive him.

Peter started off well. As long as Peter kept his eyes on Jesus, he was able to put one foot in front of another. But then he took his eyes off Jesus and focused them on the storm—the circumstances of life—and he began to sink. At that moment, Jesus had a number of options. He could've become a swim coach and suggested different strokes a frightened Peter could use to get to Him. But He didn't. Jesus remained a Savior and changed His ministry model from receiving to retrieving. He went to Peter, steadied him, and lovingly guided him back to safety.

Indeed, our churches must be equipped with a receiving model for those in church who are at risk of abortion or who are suffering from the guilt and shame of past abortions. But our churches must also have a retrieving model for those in these circumstances outside the church who may come from pregnancy centers or the broader community who, like Peter, need to be lovingly brought to safety by the hands and feet of Jesus.

As we discussed throughout this book, this is about more than just saving a baby from the atrocity of abortion. Rescuing the young woman facing an unplanned pregnancy is a natural and necessary aspect of every Christ follower's mission: to love our neighbors as ourselves and to make disciples. God may be using her unplanned pregnancy, just like he did for Mary, to call her to Him, to lead her to Jesus, and become one of His disciples. The guy who just told his girlfriend to get an abortion, or the woman who just made that decision because she felt alone and afraid, may not always walk into our churches. The enemy may tell them to stay away because what they've done makes them unwelcome there. They are afraid they won't be received, so they must be retrieved. They need a tassel.

Thank you for going on this journey with me. It's my hope that you've been informed, inspired, and encouraged to move from being pro-life to becoming pro abundant life. I pray this will be more than just an issue you align with, but that the words of this book will equip and motivate you to become a catalyst in your church or community for the pro abundant life cause. Of course, it would be impossible in a book this size to cover every nuanced aspect to issues of life, but in the chapters that follow, I offer you some situationally specific frameworks as you face people both inside and outside the church that may not agree with your pro abundant life stance. Read them all now or keep this book as a reference guide to prepare you for tricky topical conversations that arise. Each of the apologetics and frameworks are the result of years of working in this movement, seeking scripture for truth around these issues, and interacting with people of all ages and positions on issues of life. I hope they will help you as you endeavor to engage in this sacred work.

FRAMEWORK ONE

ABORTION:
Why Politics Won't Save Us

People always say, "Never discuss politics in polite company," and considering today's volatile political climate, you can't blame them. We're not at dinner or on a date, though, so I think we're safe to do it here. Let's talk politics.

If you ask some Christians if they're pro-life, many will say yes and tell you who they voted for. Don't get me wrong, this issue does have a political component. But as Christians, abortion cannot be primarily a political issue. From a pro abundant life perspective, it's primarily about living out the Great Commandment to fulfill the Great Commission.

For decades the political goal of the pro-life movement was straightforward: overturn *Roe v. Wade*. Every January, a faithful flock of devoted pro-lifers gathered in Washington, DC, to participate in a march that ended at the US Supreme Court building. Victory for those who viewed abortion primarily as a political issue would be won when the right ratio of pro-life justices was seated on the bench. Then they would rule in favor of life.

Then, in June 2022, it happened. The Supreme Court overruled both *Roe* and *Casey* (the 1992 case *Planned Parenthood v. Casey* that further broadened abortion freedoms). In *Dobbs v. Jackson Women's Health Organization*, the Supreme Court ruled the "substantive right" to abortion was not "deeply rooted in this Nation's history or tradition."[1] The court ruled the right to abortion could not have been considered a right when the due process clause was ratified in 1868 because this was unknown in US law until *Roe*.

After more than four decades of fighting abortion in the courts, it seemed pro-life supporters had won. Our celebrations were great. Sweet victory. *Victory at last.*

But did we really win? Or did we declare victory too soon?

Since the *Dobbs* decision, events have transpired that should cause us to reflect, reenergize, and act beyond the realm of politics.

The Role of Politics in Stopping Abortion

The Democratic national policy position regarding abortion has remained largely unchanged since I became the president and CEO of Care Net in 2012: abortion on demand at any time during pregnancy, for any reason, no exceptions. In fact, supporting abortion is now a litmus test for the Democratic Party. However, the Republican national policy position has changed dramatically, and the implications should transform the national dialogue around the issue of abortion.

In 2012 when Mitt Romney was the Republican nominee for president, he and the Republican Party opposed all abortions, except in cases of rape, incest, and the life of the mother.[2] This exceptions-based position would make 97 percent of abortions illegal. Furthermore, even the exceptions (though problematic in the case of rape) were evaluated through a moral lens aimed to balance compassion for the vulnerable woman harmed during conception or childbirth with the vulnerable baby harmed by the abortion procedure.

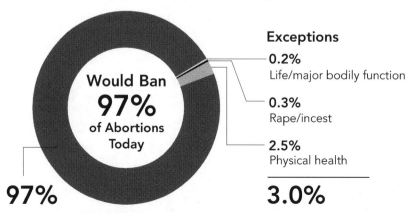

Data provided by Charlotte Lozier, *Fact Sheet: Reasons for Abortion* January 14, 2023

Today, the national Republican policy position on abortion is very different. At the time of the publication of this book, presidential candidate Donald Trump announced that, essentially, the Republican Party does not have a national position on abortion, but the issue should instead be left to "the will of the people" at the state level. Other major Republican figures have publicly supported anything from a six-week ban to a fifteen-week ban, which would include the 2012 exceptions. The most recent Centers for Disease Control and Prevention (CDC) abortion statistics indicate that a fifteen-week ban, plus the exceptions, would allow nearly 98 percent of abortions. (See chart below)

Impact of a 15-Week Abortion Ban

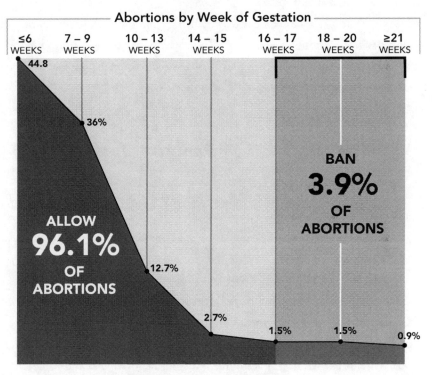

Centers for Disease Control and Prevention
Morbidity and Mortality Weekly Report Surveillance Summaries / Vol. 72 / No. 9 November 24, 2023
TABLE 14. Number and percentage of reported abortions, by known weeks of gestation, age group, and race and ethnicity — selected reporting areas, United States, 2021

Moreover, the Republican Party dramatically retreated from its pro-life position in its 2024 platform. For example, the platform no longer affirms the unborn child has a "fundamental right to life which cannot be infringed," and it abandoned the long-standing support for a Human Life Amendment to the Constitution. Although it still refers to the Fourteenth Amendment protections, by removing language asserting the unborn child is a person, this reference is hollow and moot. Finally, the only abortions the Republican platform specifically opposes are late-term abortions (generally after twenty weeks), which account for less than 2 percent of abortions.

While some states have passed stricter limits on abortion, it is clear the Republican Party's current position is starkly different from the unified 2012 Republican position. In fact, despite rhetoric on both sides, the abortion debate from a national policy perspective is no longer about bans, but rather about abortion availability.

As a result, the inconvenient truth when evaluating each party's national policy positions through the metric of saving babies in the womb from abortion is this: both parties are essentially pro-choice—one pro-choice *with no exceptions* and one pro-choice *with some exceptions.*

A Need for Steadfast Commitment to Our Convictions

In the move to a politically driven "weeks gestation-based" strategy to limit abortions, we face a further loss of commitment to the core pro-life convictions. To be clear, I am referring to two convictions: 1) human life begins at conception and is worthy of protection, and 2) the circumstances of a baby's conception and birth must not determine his or her value and worth.

Consequently, any moral or political strategy must not undermine this guiding conviction. A weeks-based argument clearly undermines this conviction because one is negotiating about when it is acceptable to kill an innocent human life in the womb. This should be as nonnegotiable as the conviction that it is wrong to kill an innocent human life outside of the womb. Simply having convictions—even the right ones—is not enough. One must have a steadfast commitment to a conviction for it to matter. If one does not commit to an action connected to a conviction, it's no better than having no conviction at all.

Ironically, the pro-choice side has not only conviction but also commitment that directs their actions, politically and otherwise. In their case, the conviction is that a woman should never be denied her bodily autonomy during pregnancy or at any time afterward. When you ask them when they would restrict or deny a woman's bodily autonomy, they say "never." It's nonnegotiable. Thus, they support abortion up until birth with no exceptions. This is why, despite how reasonable the compromise that pro-life people might offer, the pro-choice side refuses to negotiate. That's why they fought Mississippi's Gestational *Age Act* (*Dobbs*) all the way to the Supreme Court, which had a conservative majority that would likely overturn *Roe*. The Act would have prohibited abortion after fifteen weeks of pregnancy, with exceptions for medical emergencies and fetal abnormalities, and would allow nearly 98 percent of abortions.

The pro-life movement's approach of negotiation based on weeks of gestation has a fatal flaw in a moral, political, and practical sense. First, from a moral perspective, it's an incremental approach that undermines the baby's personhood and the sanctity of life, because we are negotiating on when it's acceptable to kill a vulnerable life in the womb. This is very different from the ban on partial birth abortion, an incremental approach that affirmed the baby's humanity by prohibiting a very heinous act. Second, from a political and practical perspective, our goal is to inspire more people to adopt the pro-life conviction about the protection of life in the womb. Compromising on conviction does not move people toward adopting those convictions. I can't think of a single successful religious, political, or social movement where this approach has worked.

Compromising on conviction does not move people toward adopting those convictions. I can't think of a single successful religious, political, or social movement where this approach has worked.

Consider the issue of slavery, which is often referenced as a parallel to the fight against abortion. Before the Civil War, people like Abraham Lincoln were antislavery. In 1859 Lincoln said, "I think slavery is wrong, morally and politically."[3] Despite this, he focused on stemming the spread of slavery rather than abolishing it. In his first inaugural address he said, "I have no purpose, directly or indirectly, to interfere with the institution of slavery in the States where it exists."[4] He was willing to compromise on his conviction that slavery was morally wrong and negotiate with the southern states. This is similar to a weeks-based ban approach that does not seek to end abortion, but rather stop it from spreading beyond fifteen weeks. Although Lincoln had a conviction, the conviction was not linked to actions that would accomplish the conviction.

Abolitionists like Frederick Douglass had the same conviction as the antislavery folks. Both groups believed slavery was politically and morally wrong. However, the abolitionists' conviction was linked to a commitment to end slavery at all costs. They rightly believed this was a logical and consistent outcome for their conviction. They were not willing to compromise on their conviction and linked their actions and strategies to this conviction.

So, what happened? Douglass consistently engaged Lincoln based on their shared conviction, challenging Lincoln to take further action. Their shared convictions would demand the action to free all slaves everywhere. Over time, the weight and moral clarity of Douglass's commitment to his convictions had a powerful impact on Lincoln. By the end of the Civil War, it was inconceivable for Lincoln to have a union that included the institution of slavery. Lincoln's second inaugural speech reflects this shift because he made no reference to ending the "terrible war" to preserve the union. Moreover, he saw the Civil War as a God-ordained "woe due" to those by whom the moral offense of slavery came into the nation.[5]

In Lincoln and Douglass's final meeting after the speech was given, Lincoln asked Douglass what he thought of the speech. When Douglass demurred, Lincoln told him, "There is no man in the country whose opinion I value more than yours."[6]

In a moral and political sense, people in the pro-life movement want pro-life politicians to have the moral clarity of Abraham Lincoln. When we cosign a weeks-based framework to limit abortion for political expediency, our lack of commitment to our core convictions does not inspire moral and political courage, nor does it inspire or persuade the broader culture that we embrace our convictions. Without a willingness to act like Frederick Douglass, you will rarely get a politician to act like Abraham Lincoln.

Pilate's Dilemma and the Way Forward

I acknowledge and appreciate that many Republican politicians at all government levels are deeply pro-life. They speak forcefully for the cause of life and are working earnestly to put policies and initiatives in place to support women at risk for abortion. Moreover, I'm thankful for the significant work done to make the *Dobbs* decision to overturn *Roe v. Wade* a reality.

However, if the national pro-life policy position is either nonexistent or tolerant of a framework that allows nearly 98 percent of abortions, then the impact of the rhetoric and past efforts will be muted and short-lived. Indeed, embracing the current policy position cedes the abortion issue to the pro-choice side before there is chance for debate. There is no doubt Democrats would not consider politicians to be pro-choice if they indicated we should

> *However, if the national pro-life policy position is either nonexistent or tolerant of a framework that allows nearly 98 percent of abortions, then the impact of the rhetoric and past efforts will be muted and short-lived.*

"leave it up to the states," or if they embraced a policy position that allowed abortion in just 2 to 3 percent of cases.

Political dynamics are obviously at play here. But one needs to be clear regarding the foundation of the abortion debate. It seeks to answer the question, "When is it acceptable for the powerful to take the life of the vulnerable, for the sake of the powerful?" When considering this important question, every politician is faced with the same dilemma that Pontius Pilate faced when he sent an innocent man, Jesus, to His death.

Should the shouts of a powerful and vocal crowd sway a politician to concede, even if it means the innocent are sacrificed? It takes Lincoln-like moral clarity to resist these voices. After all, the politics of abortion do not change the morality of what happens in an abortion. In the 2012 presidential election season, the Republican Party had a measure of moral clarity, and I remain hopeful that it can be regained. Moreover, I fervently hope the Democratic Party can gain moral clarity, because vulnerable lives in the womb are at risk.

Given the reality that the two major political party positions on abortion are increasingly less divergent, where should Christians expend their pro-life energy? I do not think we should abandon the political process. We still have a duty to call for just laws that protect the innocent, and to align our moral positions with our political positions as much as possible.

In a political context, when Christ stood before Pilate it taught us three things: the limits of politics; the danger of politicians who don't prioritize truth; and the power of the crowd. It's important to remember that Jesus never expected Pilate to save Him. When questioned by Pilate, the crowd shouted for the release of the criminal Barabbas, not the innocent Jesus. Pilate the politician, who was not interested in truth, gave them Barabbas. If we want to change the decisions that politicians make, we have to change the crowd.

A common aphorism is that culture is upstream from politics. However, as Richard John Neuhaus aptly stated, politics is a function of culture, and culture is a reflection of, if not a function of, religion.[7] In other words, if you lose the pews, you lose at the polls. And if you lose the pastors, you lose the pews. This is exactly what we have seen with the abortion issue. Consider the 2023 Ohio ballot initiative to amend the Constitution to make abortion a right in the state. Ohio is considered to be a pro-life state, but the initiative passed with nearly 57 percent voting yes.[8] Based on the exit poll data, when you consider both Catholics and Protestants, the percentage that voted yes was in the range of the broader culture. We lost the pews and we lost at the polls. Frankly, we should not be surprised at this outcome because 54 percent of women who have abortions profess to be Catholic or Protestant.[9]

While I agree we need to reach the broader culture on the abortion issue, we also need to urgently prioritize our pro abundant life time, talent, and treasure on a specific segment of culture—Christians.

Consider again Jesus standing before Pontius Pilate. Now, imagine you are a follower of Jesus in the crowd standing before Pilate. Of course, you are yelling with all your might, "Jesus!" in response to Pilate's query. But your voice is being drowned out by the crowd yelling "Barabbas!" Clearly, you need to change the crowd, but how? Out of the corner of your eye, you see Bartimaeus, the formerly blind beggar that Jesus gave sight. To your surprise, he is yelling "Barabbas!" He has clearly wandered from the way, the truth, and the life.

You go to him and ask, "Why are you yelling Barabbas?" He sheepishly looks at you and says, "Well, everyone else was…" You then remind Bartimaeus that he knows Jesus and what Jesus did for him—how Jesus lived out the Great Commandment, loving him sacrificially, to fulfill the Great Commission in his life. Bartimaeus responds, "You're right!" And then begins to yell "Jesus!" And then, you see the woman with the issue of blood, and she is yelling "Barabbas!" too. So, you head toward her.

The way forward when dealing with moral issues like abortion has never changed. Yet so much of our effort on the abortion issue is to persuade "Pilate" to save us or try to reach the broad crowd of unbelievers. Jesus said the gates of hell, which abortion represents, will not prevail against the church. Indeed, his church must lead on the abortion issue in word and ministry deed. That's why when Jesus came, he didn't start with just anyone in the "crowd." He started with the people of the Book who *should* know him. As followers of Christ, we must follow his example as our way forward. We must start by reaching our pews and removing the log in our eye to clearly see how to reach our lost culture. While that seems like a monumental task, by God's grace and with focus, it's achievable.

Download a free digital copy of Framework One by scanning the QR code below:

FRAMEWORK TWO

ENGAGING A
PRO-CHOICE PERSON:
Why It's Important to Find Common Ground

Engaging a pro-choice person in a discussion about abortion is very difficult. Regardless of whether the person is a family member, friend, or work colleague, these conversations too often end up as shouting matches that reflect more heat than light. Considering this challenge, I am reminded of Jesus's advice to His disciples when He sent them out in pairs to proclaim the gospel to a hostile world. He told them that if folks didn't want to listen to the truth, move on and shake the dust from their feet (Matthew 10:14). In the face of an argument about abortion, it's tempting to implement this approach too quickly. We must learn to endure some discomfort in order to share truth.

To properly discern who to engage in discussion, think about the abortion debate as a normal distribution curve. On the tail ends, you have folks who are solid in their pro-choice and pro-life convictions. However, most people are somewhere on the hump. I refer to these people as potentially "pro-choice lite." Accordingly, I believe they can be reached by the power of the Holy Spirit with a thoughtful and winsome approach.

Several years ago, a Care Net Ministry Partner invited a friend to join a meeting with me because he thought he would be interested in the ministry. After he gave a brief introduction to Care Net's work and me, the guy looked at me and said in a very stern tone, "So you don't think a woman should have control of her own body, do you?" Alas, it was clear this man was not on the same side of the abortion debate as my Ministry Partner and me.

The usual pro-life response would be that we are not talking about the woman's body, but rather another separate and distinct human life in the woman's body. However, by God's leading, rather than responding with that answer, I responded with a question seeking to better understand his position before I tried to get him to understand mine. I said, "It sounds like you are pro-choice, right?" He said, "Yes!" Not only was he pro-choice, but his business did work for Planned Parenthood and his daughter had worked there!

I said to him, "OK, so the two choices are birth and abortion, and you don't care which decision a woman makes, as long as she has the right to make it, right?" He nodded in agreement. Then I asked if there were any obstacles from conception until birth to stop the woman from having an abortion, would he want to remove those obstacles and he said, "Yes!"

Then, I tore a piece of paper out of my notebook and drew a circle with a line that divided the circle in half. On the left side of the line, I wrote the word "abortion" and on the right side I wrote the word "birth." I put the letter C at the top of line for conception and put a B at the bottom of the line for birth (See Diagram A).

DIAGRAM A

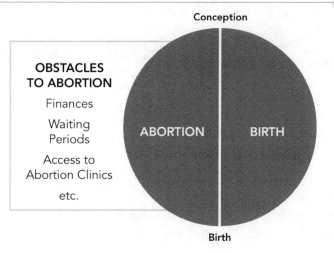

Outside the abortion side of the circle, I wrote obstacles a woman could face to having an abortion, like finances, waiting periods, access to facilities, etc. Then I said, "You want to remove all these obstacles and others," and he said, "Absolutely!" Then, I wrote the word obstacles on the side of the circle next to the word birth and said, "Now, of course, you want to work just as hard to remove the obstacles to birth as well…correct?" (You see, to be *truly* pro-choice, you must be just as committed to removing obstacles to birth as you are to removing obstacles to abortion.) He paused for a moment, and then said, "Well, yes." So, I began to list obstacles connected to the missing support needed by a woman at risk for abortion.

Next, I drew a second circle and put the word birth in the middle of it and put a C at the top and the B at the bottom like I did with the other circle. I wrote obstacles next to it and listed the same ones that I did next to the birth side of his circle (See Diagram B). Then, I told him this represented my pro-life position. I, too, wanted to support women from conception to birth who wanted to have their babies but are facing obstacles. I told him that is what Care Net's affiliated pregnancy centers do—find ways to remove these obstacles to birth to support a woman's birth choice.

DIAGRAM B

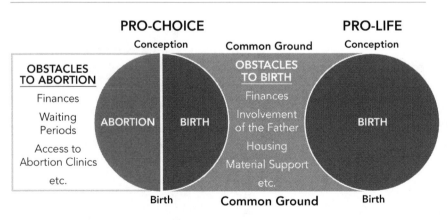

I paused for a moment, like the detective Columbo used to do, and said, "Looks like we have common ground." I then drew a circle to connect my circle to the birth part of his pro-choice circle.

When you're trying to find common ground with someone, it helps to follow a few ground rules. For example, if you're going out to dinner with a vegan, don't take them to a steak house. You wouldn't say, "Here's a compromise: you have just a little bit of steak." No, the common ground between the omnivore and the vegan is at the salad bar. The salad bar is figuratively the birth side of the equation.

Often you will hear pro-choice people challenge pro-life people with the obligation to care for children that result from a life-affirming decision. Their position is that supporting these children is a specific obligation only for pro-lifers. But if they are truly pro-choice, they have just as much of an obligation to support these children, because these little ones are the result of a woman's choice. Although pro-life people have no obligation to remove the obstacles to birth, pro-choice people have the obligation to remove the obstacles to birth, from conception to birth, and to support the result of a woman's life-affirming choice—her child.

In any case, he agreed there was common ground between our positions. I spent the remainder of our time together explaining what pregnancy centers do and encouraged him to visit one. Most pro-choice people don't have outlets to enlighten the birth side of their worldview, and pregnancy centers give them that ability. I am keenly aware that as a pro-choice person begins to "taste and see" women in difficult circumstances empowered to choose life, it will grow the birth side of their circle. During my conversation, what clearly could have devolved into an argument became a conversation where seeds of life were planted in this man's heart and mind. In fact, the last thing he did as we left the meeting was give me his business card.

The reason I call those who support abortion pro-choice rather than pro-abortion is to help them see they do have a life aspect to their worldview. Granted, there are some, like Margaret Sanger, who are truly pro-abortion because they believe in controlling a woman's choice based on factors such as her race and economic situation. But most pro-choice people don't think this way. So, when we call them pro-abortion, it often misrepresents their position, and we miss an important opportunity to engage them.

Transformation in thinking rarely occurs without conversation. Every person who was once pro-choice and became pro-life had a revelation.

Something triggered the birth side of their pro-choice circle to grow so much that the abortion side was eclipsed. I know this sounds counterintuitive, but the first step in getting a pro-choice person to become pro-life is to help them understand the life-affirming obligation embedded in their pro-choice position.

Here's another way to think about this. My wife Yvette is an avid gardener, and often she plants ground cover next to a stone pathway. I've noticed that with some watering, the ground cover grows and covers the stone pathway. But the pathway never overtakes the ground cover, despite it getting water too. Why? Because the ground cover is alive, and the stone pathway is dead. God sets before everyone life and death (Deuteronomy 30:19). The birth side of a pro-choice person's worldview is alive and the abortion aspect is dead. Like my gardener wife Yvette, our calling is to apply the living water of the Holy Spirit to a pro-choice person's worldview so it can grow. Amen!

Download a free digital copy of Framework Two by scanning the QR code below:

FRAMEWORK THREE

COMPASSION PAIRING™:
How to Answer Those Who Believe Abortion Is a Compassionate Choice

Remember Mary Elizabeth Williams from chapter three, the woman who wrote the article titled, "So What if Abortion Ends a Life?"[1] If we're honest, Mary Elizabeth Williams isn't doing anything out of the ordinary. She's simply determining who deserves the most compassion. This paradigm isn't new; follow me on an uncomfortable journey to see how this compassion paradigm has frequently been used throughout history.

Let's take Williams's statement, "I would put the life of a mother over the life of a fetus every single time," but let's replace those words "mother" and "fetus" to realize how we've seen this play out before. First, let's replace those words with "Nazi" and "Jew." I doubt anyone in 1940s Germany questioned that the Jewish people were fully alive and human. Yet the Nazis believed that Jewish lives were worth sacrificing for the sake of their own world-conquering goals.

How about replacing those words with "slave owner" and "slave." It then reads, "I would put the life of a slave owner over the life of a slave every single time, even if I still need to acknowledge my conviction that a slave is indeed a life. It is a life worth sacrificing." Whoa. I hope you see my point. In China, they used the terms "baby boy" and "baby girl" in their quest for a male-dominated society. It's not uncommon to see the able-bodied valued more than the disabled or the elderly. The worldview reflected in Williams's statement is the same worldview held by everyone who has committed some of the most heinous acts and cruelest violence in the history of mankind.

We can no longer effectively champion the pro-life cause by solely trying to prove that a fetus is a life. There's a bigger, more powerful worldview at play.

Compassion Pairings™

The worldview Mary Elizabeth Williams likely doesn't recognize she holds makes a statement about how the powerful will interact with and treat the vulnerable. We dress this stuff up with law and language. We disguise the truth with words like "solution," as in "final solution," and "choice," and mantras like the Clintons touted in the 1994 election about abortion being "safe, legal, and rare." But when you undress the language and show the naked truth, it's the language of death to those who cannot protect themselves.

This is why we object to abortion with such passion. We understand this, don't we? Moreover, we serve the Lamb. What did we learn from His compelling example? We learned exactly how the powerful are supposed to interact with and treat the vulnerable. We know from Philippians 2 that Christ clothed Himself in humanity. When He died on the cross with His arms open wide, He demonstrated a powerful point. The powerful must not sacrifice the vulnerable for themselves. They must sacrifice themselves for the vulnerable.

Three words are critical to Care Net's work and ultimately the pro abundant life message. These words are: power, vulnerability, and compassion. First, let's unpack the concept of power. Power is an ability to act in a particular way or the capability to direct yourself or someone else. When people have power, they can direct themselves and influence or control others.

Vulnerability is the flip side of power. It's the lack of an ability to do something or act in a particular way. It's the lack of capacity to influence someone else. Vulnerable people are more susceptible to those who are powerful. There's an interplay between power and vulnerability. Other than God, no one is all powerful. Likewise, no one is all vulnerable. Depending on the situation, you may be more powerful or more vulnerable. There's a fluidity between the two concepts.

Now let's talk about compassion. Compassion is a notion of sympathetic concern or care for someone else. It denotes a focus on others that leads to righteousness and justice. That's a big part of what we do at Care Net—we are purveyors of compassion in our work.

Let's look at the interplay between these three concepts: power, vulnerability, and compassion. The question is, who do we have the most compassion for, the powerful or the vulnerable? Most of us tend to be more compassionate for the vulnerable. We like to root for the underdog. It's almost like a definition of humanity.

Herein lies a conundrum. Compassion is a commodity that must be apportioned. All day long, we make decisions about how to allocate compassion. You hear about it in decisions about government health care, housing, homelessness, and more. Many conversations revolve around compassion. How do we apportion it? And what's the framework to use when trying to apportion compassion?

I came up with a simple way to better understand this paradigm. I call it Compassion Pairing™ (CP), and it's a way to help us understand the powerful role of compassion in the abortion debate. Imagine you're watching a nature documentary. The scene shows a lovely gazelle grazing in the field and a hungry, ferocious lion. In this pairing, it's easy to see which animal is powerful and which is vulnerable. The lion will easily overpower the vulnerable gazelle. So where does our compassion land? Watch the nature show with a group of people and someone will surely cry out, "Awww! No!" as the gazelle becomes the lion's lunch. Our compassion often follows the vulnerable.

Earlier we touched on another example. The Jews in concentration camps and the Nazis who put them there. Who's more powerful? Who's more vulnerable? It's pretty clear to see. Or what about comparing two different women. One is drinking a bottle of Evian, the other's drinking dirty stream water. Who is the more powerful? Who is the more vulnerable?

We could go through these pairings all day. Compare the bodybuilder to a baby. Picture an elderly woman versus a twenty-something jogging the trail. In so many situations we can imagine, it's easy to distinguish the powerful from the vulnerable. Though we may be impressed by the powerful, our compassion usually follows the vulnerable.

Let's specifically consider the CP framework in the context of abortion. To start, imagine you are in a restaurant with a friend who is eight months pregnant, and she orders alcohol. Do you have a problem? Yes. Why? Because your mind automatically did a quick CP analysis that identified the more powerful (the woman) and the more vulnerable (her unborn baby). You quickly apportioned more of your compassion toward the vulnerable baby. And here's the thing: a pro-choice person would very likely agree with you and have a problem with your friend drinking alcohol.

So how does the pro-choice person end up with a divergent viewpoint when a woman gets on the surgical table for an abortion or takes the abortion pill? It's good to remember Scripture says our battle is not against flesh and blood, but against Satan's forces of evil in the heavenly realms (Ephesians 6:11–20). In short, the evil one skillfully uses several techniques to short-circuit the CP framework that God wired into humanity.

COMPASSION PAIRING™
How Do You Apportion Compassion?

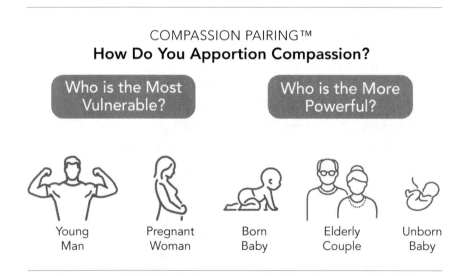

| Who is the Most Vulnerable? | Who is the More Powerful? |

| Young Man | Pregnant Woman | Born Baby | Elderly Couple | Unborn Baby |

First, he tempts us to dehumanize one of the pair. This is exactly what happened with abortion when the baby in the womb was considered just a blob of cells. In fact, this is what happened with the Jews in the Holocaust and Black people during slavery. When the vulnerable are dehumanized, injustice is frequently a result.

Second, Satan tempts us to use a different CP and apply it to another situation. For example, you often hear pro-choice politicians make statements like, "I support a woman's right to choose, and I don't think a bunch of men should be controlling her choice." In this case, the CP is between men and women, and since women are generally viewed as more vulnerable than men, they get more compassion. They are using the woman/man CP and applying it to the abortion decision.

Finally, Satan tempts us to focus on the situation rather than the people in the situation, generally through story or narrative. For example, some try to focus on the situation and say the baby is more powerful than the woman because the baby can change her life. However, abortion is framed as a woman's empowerment issue (My Body, My Choice!). Clearly the one who can end another's life is more powerful than the one who can change another's life. Getting drawn into the emotions of the narrative makes it very easy to lose sight of the facts of the situation. In the case of abortion, a vulnerable human life is being sacrificed for the powerful—a framework that compassionate people consistently reject as unjust.

Given the horror of abortion, it might be easy to think those on the pro-choice side have no compassion. But generally, that is not true. Pro-choice people are mis-apportioning compassion in a way that they don't in other situations. Therefore, a great way to engage them is to model your approach after the apostle Paul in his efforts to reach the Athenians, who worshipped an unknown God (Acts 17:22–34). Paul used the common ground of worship and skillfully introduced the truth of the gospel of Jesus Christ. Some mocked him. However, others said they wanted to hear about Jesus again, and some joined him and believed.

In the case of abortion, the common ground with pro-choice people can be compassion. Imagine if you started the conversation with a pro-choice person with, "I know that you are a compassionate person," and then give examples of CP scenarios: Who's the more powerful? Who's the more vulnerable? How do you apportion compassion? This allows you to find some common ground. Then, like Paul, you can show them they are apportioning compassion in abortion differently than they do in every other situation, and then encourage them to join you. A truly compassionate person, regardless of the circumstances, does not sacrifice the vulnerable for the powerful.

The CP model is so central to the human condition that God used it to facilitate our redemption through Jesus Christ. Specifically, God used power, vulnerability, and compassion to bring Jesus into the world. Jesus emptied himself of His power and increased His vulnerability by clothing Himself in the flesh of humanity (Philippians 2). He came into the world as a vulnerable baby, and He left the world with His arms wide open, beaten, bloody, and exposed—vulnerable. In our humanity, we cannot help but be drawn to Him and have compassion for Him.

Download a free digital copy of Framework Three by scanning the QR code below:

FRAMEWORK FOUR

WHAT TO SAY TO SOMEONE WHO IS PRO-LIFE EXCEPT IN CASES OF RAPE

I am not the "rapist's child." I was her child. I am God's child. I'm one of thousands, every year, given the opportunity to live, love, and redeem what the rapist tried to destroy. Our stories are full of hope, full of love, full of purpose.

—Ryan Bomberger

One of the most difficult questions to address in the abortion debate is the situation of rape. Pro-life author and speaker Ryan Bomberger, who was conceived in rape and placed for adoption, notes it's the scenario that is used often to justify making abortion available in all situations.

Abortion in cases of rape actually account for about 1 percent of abortions.[1] While statistically accurate, that figure is no comfort for the woman who was raped. She is a victim deserving of the utmost compassion. I have a wife, sisters, daughters-in-law, nieces, granddaughters, and countless other women I love dearly, and the thought of them being violated in this way is difficult for me to even contemplate. I understand the desire to "make things right" by having an exception in this case. But the circumstances of a baby's conception and birth must not determine its value and worth. That's why we no longer call children who are born out of wedlock illegitimate or bastards. Ryan Bomberger is a committed husband and father of four children who is doing lifesaving work in this world. Is his existence less worthy because of how he was conceived? I think not.

Yet it's been tricky for the pro-life movement to articulate this viewpoint in a way that doesn't sound narrow-minded or, candidly, just cruel. Using the Compassion Pairing™ (CP) concept I mentioned in framework three, you can better understand why some pro-life and pro-choice people make this exception, and how to respond persuasively to make the case for the life of the baby in the womb as result of rape.

My thoughts about the CP framework as it relates to instances of rape were challenged by a conversation with a young Christian college student who liked to debate tough issues like abortion. I asked her to tell me her understanding of the pro-choice position, and she responded that "they don't believe it's a life," along with a few other key arguments. Then I asked about the pro-life arguments.

"We believe that life begins at conception."

"OK, but what do you say to people who are pro-life, except in cases of rape?"

"I would say to them that life begins at conception."

"Yes—they agree with you that life begins at conception. Then what would you say?"

"Well…I'd just keep telling them that."

The more I thought more about her response, the clearer it became that we need better answers. I wondered how someone can be pro-life, except in cases of rape—what is going on in that person's head? I determined that it has to do with power, vulnerability, and compassion. It's about how they configure CP in this situation.

Remember, the CP paradigm is about how we apportion compassion. It's the human condition that naturally occurs, almost without thinking about it. For example, let's once again pair the woman and the baby to assign power, vulnerability, and compassion. Who's the more powerful? Obviously, the woman. Who's the more vulnerable? Again, clearly the baby. I'm not saying the woman has no vulnerability. And I'm also not saying the baby has no power. It's fluid. The baby has some power and the woman has some vulnerability.

In the scenario of rape, however, someone changes the CP. Those who support abortion in cases of rape no longer compare the baby to the woman to make the decision. They compare the woman to her rapist. In this matchup, they understandably assign more power to the rapist and more vulnerability to the woman. Therefore, they have more compassion for her.

This situation is similar to the one I discussed in framework three, where pro-choice people use the CP of men/women to support abortion. In this case, people are using the rapist/woman CP to support the abortion of the baby. But in reality, that's not really what's going on in the undeniably difficult case of rape. If conception occurs because of rape, the woman should move into the CP where she is matched to the baby. The rapist then moves into a new CP, where it's the rapist versus the justice system.

Between the rapist and the justice system, who's more powerful? Who's more vulnerable? Where's our compassion? I know it almost breaks your brain. Based on our justice system, our compassion is for the rapist because constitutionally he's "innocent until proven guilty." That's justice. It's a form of compassion. It's our legal system. It's a reflection of compassion.

Compassion Pairing™ happens in lots of situations. Let's compare the people with disabilities and those without disabilities. Who's the more powerful? Those without disability. Who's the more vulnerable? Those with disability. How do you apportion compassion? Toward the people living with a disability.

The only way to change this scenario is to introduce a backstory—the key factor that can decrease power and increase vulnerability. Have you ever watched a movie and halfway through you realize you're cheering for the bad guy? You're like, "Oh, he's just killed twelve people. Please let him get away!"

How does that happen? The character is clearly rotten, but then there's a flashback. It shows the character being abused as a small boy. And suddenly, your compassion is with the villain. You understand him better. Your heart goes out to him. Isn't this also what happens before sentencing a criminal? A good lawyer gives the backstory. They play with power, vulnerability, and compassion. It's a truism of life. It happens everywhere.

Now let's look at the pro-choice position and use the same argument. You have the woman; you have the baby. The pro-choice logic is that the baby is more powerful and the woman is more vulnerable, so she should have our compassion.

Let's say I'm a lion on the Serengeti and I'm trying to decide what's for lunch. I've got an adult gazelle, and I've got a baby gazelle. I do a power, vulnerability, and compassion assessment. Who's the more powerful? The adult gazelle, of course. Who's the more vulnerable? The baby gazelle. So, who do I attack? I go for the easier prey. I choose the baby gazelle. So, in this case, my compassion is apportioned to the adult gazelle. I let the adult go free and have the baby for lunch.

Have you ever watched a Disney movie that tries to make an animal seem human? The storytellers use power, vulnerability, and compassion to humanize the animal characters. This works because in real life, the difference between animals and people is that animals prey on the vulnerable and people protect the vulnerable. What defines humanity is how we interact with power, vulnerability, and compassion. This is why people who are for abortion often don't want to talk about it—because it's a violation of our humanity.

But Babies Do Change Everything

Some on the pro-choice side may say that my assessment here is wrong. They do believe the baby is more powerful than the woman because the baby has the power to change her life—to change everything. There's even a baby products commercial that says it: "Babies change everything."

To their position, I pose a scenario. Let's say you're in a restaurant with an adjacent bar. You see a woman sitting at the bar who is smoking and drinking. Is there a problem with that? Of course not. No one is going to stop her if she's of legal age. But let me add to our scenario. The woman at the bar is obviously pregnant, due any day now. Does that change anything? Of course it does. We'd all be concerned because she's going to hurt her baby. We would wonder how she didn't know this is wrong. The brave among us would be glad to tap her on the shoulder and let her know the damage she is causing.

When we assess the pregnant woman drinking and smoking, we quickly apportion the power, vulnerability, and compassion paradigm of the situation. We don't even think about it. It just happens.

How do you think someone who's pro-choice would react to the woman in the bar versus a woman who is pregnant as a result of rape? Would they consider how the vulnerable baby in the bar becomes suddenly more powerful in the abortion room?

The variable is the backstory—the situation. But changing the situation doesn't change the reality. The essence of humanity does not change situationally. The fact that I'm a person or not a person doesn't change based on my situation.

A false CP muddied the abortion debate. They pitted women against men and then encouraged evaluation. Who's more powerful? Who's more vulnerable? This became the core of their argument. If you've ever heard a politician say something like, "I think a woman should have the right to choose, and I don't think a bunch of men here in Washington should be making that decision," they're using a CP to defend their opinion. This is the feminist narrative. It's men versus women. But therein lies our opportunity.

When I talk to people who say these things, I'm quick to explain that I know why they believe what they believe. Whenever you see the powerful taking advantage of the vulnerable, your compassion is ignited. Then I explain that this is exactly why I'm pro-life. We have a consistent narrative they don't see.

The False Compassion Pairing™

Our power, vulnerability, and compassion framework disappears once we're no longer comparing two people. If the CP is between a human and a thing, the human will win the compassion every time. Pro-choice advocates maintain the false CP that makes abortion seem like the most compassionate option. They say, "This issue is not about a woman and a baby. It's about a woman and a question mark. A thing."

If we want something to be protected, we humanize it. Think about how animal rights proponents use power, vulnerability, and compassion. Television commercials portray a poor, cold, hungry animal with its mangy mess of hair and a sad look on its face, with moody Sarah McLachlan music playing in the background. It's designed to make you feel compassion for that animal and anger toward any human who mistreated it.

Let's consider a CP that compares the rapist to the baby. Where's the power? Where's the vulnerability? Who dies in this worldview? Do you see what happened? If we stand for abortion in cases of rape, then it's the baby who dies in this matchup. This worldview actually holds more compassion for the rapist.

Here's something else that's interesting to think about. Why don't we allow women who have been raped to sit on their attacker's jury? We would say the woman who was raped is too close to the situation. She can't choose what happens to the rapist. That wouldn't be justice.

Now think of that same woman carrying a child because of rape. Which is she closest to, the rapist or the baby? We know that if you're too close to the situation, it's difficult for you to be just—that's why that decision wasn't left to us. That's why that situation was left for God.

What is it about rape that we find so abhorrent? It's because someone used their power against someone more vulnerable. You see, the same reason we have such disdain for rape is the same reason we must reject abortion. Interestingly, when I have heard the compelling stories of compassionate and courageous women who were raped and yet gave birth, they are rejecting abortion for this reason. Specifically, they refuse to let the rapist extend his power through them to the little one in their womb by having an abortion. Indeed, they are motivated by a CP between their baby and the rapist in which they have the most compassion for the most vulnerable. When they bring their baby into the world, they are modeling the same sacrificial love Jesus exhibited on the cross. In the midst of their pain, these courageous women have the moral clarity to see the vulnerable ones who need their sacrifice. And that is why their children call their birth mothers blessed.

Download a free digital copy of Framework Four by scanning the QR code below:

FRAMEWORK FIVE

HOW TO RESPOND WHEN TOLD THAT MEN SHOULD HAVE NO SAY IN THE ABORTION DECISION

If you've been around the abortion debate for any period of time, you've probably heard someone say that men's opinions, thoughts, and actions about abortion don't matter. The position—typically held by pro-choice people—argues that since a man does not have a womb to carry an unborn child, he should have no moral, legal, or ethical say in what happens to an unborn child. They have framed abortion as a woman's issue through the "My Body, My Choice" mantra, and they just want men to stay out of it. Care Net hears this challenge to men so often we've coined it the "no womb, no say" perspective.

Some years ago, the pro-choice movement started an aggressive initiative encouraging men to support abortion rights. This effort challenged men to be "Bro-choice," and even took pledges to show their support. In fact, in 2015 the Men4Choice initiative was started.[1] Unite for Reproductive and Gender Equity (URGE), another major proponent of the Bro-choice movement, states on its website, "Pro-choice men can be a powerful force in helping move our policy agenda forward, which is exactly why URGE leads the way in recruiting and elevating their voices within this movement."[2]

Most recently, Second Gentleman Doug Emhoff, husband of Vice President Kamala Harris, convened a panel discussion that focused on the role men can play in championing more access to abortion rights. The panel was co-hosted by Men4Choice. Moreover, *The Wall Street Journal* recently printed a glowing story about recruitment efforts targeting men to support a woman's bodily autonomy.[3] Oddly, the publication was nowhere to be found when Care Net hosted two first of their kind and well-attended Called and Missioned pro-life men's conferences.

After reading these perspectives, I was reminded of the old quip, "When I want your opinion, I will give it to you." It also reminded me of a pro-choice bumper sticker that says, "I don't want my reproductive rights decided by a bunch of gray-haired white guys." Of course, this bumper sticker misses the irony that abortion was made legal by just such a group—the Supreme Court in 1973. If old white guys can't get it right now, isn't it possible they got it wrong then? In any case, for Bro-choice advocates it's perfectly fine for men to engage in the abortion debate, as long as they come down on the right side.

That hypocrisy aside, let's take a closer look at the "no womb, no say" perspective and see if it holds up to scrutiny. First let's start with the obvious: men are one-half of the biological equation when it comes to creating a pregnancy, so to argue they have nothing of value to say about the fate of that pregnancy is a logical stretch.

Second, the principle underlying the "no womb, no say" view is that unless one is impacted by an issue in the most direct way, one should have no agency in making decisions about that issue. So, let's consider a few situations. Should a woman who is a stay-at-home mom and makes no income outside the home have a say on tax policy? After all, she doesn't directly pay taxes on an income. Should someone who does not own a gun have a say in our nation's gun laws? A non-gun owner is not going to be directly impacted if access to guns is limited.

When you consider the "no womb, no say" perspective in light of our nation's history, it's especially troubling. Consider the Civil War. The South was primarily an agrarian society structured around and dependent on slave labor. Indeed, a key aspect of the Southern states' rights argument was that since the North's society and economic system would not have been directly impacted by the abolition of slavery, the North should have no say. Indeed, "no slaves, no say," was the South's proverbial battle cry.

Consider the issue of voting rights in the United States. From our nation's founding, voting rights were limited to property-owning or tax-paying white males who made up about 6 percent of the population. So the notion was, "no property, no say."

Even when voting rights were extended to other men, women were still excluded. Why? Because many men believed women should not be directly involved in the economic and civil aspects of American society. Consequently, these men held a "womb, no say" perspective when it came to voting rights. The women's suffrage movement rightly changed that perspective, and with the passage of the Nineteenth Amendment to the Constitution in 1920, women were given the right to vote…by men. All these examples prove we have rightly rejected the principle that undergirds the "no womb, no say" perspective on abortion.

When considering what is best for our society, we don't consider only the view of those directly impacted to the exclusion of all others. To do so would be an injustice, especially to those who are vulnerable. Rather, we give an equal say and even encourage the voices of those who are affected, even if it's only indirectly.

Indeed, a stay-at-home mom is affected by tax policy, so she has an equal right and is encouraged to vote. Our nation's gun laws affect the safety of the communities where the non-gun owners live and raise their children, so they must have an equal say in the enacted laws. The moral stain and injustice of slavery affected those in the North, so they had agency and an obligation to fight a bloody war to eliminate it. The laws passed in this nation affected women's rights to life, liberty, and the pursuit of happiness, so it was an injustice to deny them the right to vote.

In all these issues, our society determined it would be an injustice to deny certain people the right to have a say in issues that affect them, even if indirectly. Men are directly impacted by pregnancies they create. Several recent studies have confirmed the reality that abortion does affect men. One study found five different ways in which men were affected by abortion, such as expressing a need for counseling and experiencing ambivalent and painful emotions after abortion. When an unborn child is killed in the womb it deeply affects a man, especially if it is his child. So doesn't it make sense for him to have a say too?

Download a free digital copy of Framework Five by scanning the QR code below:

APOLOGETIC:

IS THE PRO-CHOICE POSITION CONSISTENT WITH THE LIFE AND TEACHINGS OF JESUS CHRIST?

Throughout this book, I have expounded on the need to reach Christians who profess to be pro-choice. However, given the urgent need to address this challenge, below is a comprehensive four-part apologetic framework based on the words and life of Jesus to use in your discussions. Also, I encourage you to visit Care Net's website to order copies of the booklet, "Is the Pro-Choice Position Consistent with the Life and Teachings of Jesus Christ?" You can also use the QR code or go to www.resources.care-net.org/pro-choice-christians-ebook/ to get a free downloadable PDF.

Is the Pro-Choice Position Consistent with the Life and Teachings of Jesus Christ?

This is a critical discussion at this moment in our nation's and the church's history because it is very clear that there is disunity in the Christian community regarding the life issue. The evil one and injustice always thrive in such an environment. Moreover, it is not just enough that Christians are pro-life, but that they also understand why they are pro-life. There are those who are pro-life because of personal politics or family traditions. There are also those who feel called to provide material support for women in need. But the "why" for our pro-life position must be firmly anchored in the gospel of Jesus Christ. The gospel alone provides the most biblically durable and steadfast reasoning for the pro-life position. Only with the gospel is our pro-life conviction capable of weathering the challenges of life, the storms of circumstances, and the press of temptation. It is important for each one of us to proactively become ambassadors for the unborn to our pro-choice Christian brothers and sisters. The book of James reminds us that if a brother or sister "wanders from the truth," we should seek to bring them back. So, I want to equip you to lovingly have these conversations. Indeed, you are uniquely positioned to have these vital conversations because you are in relationships with pro-choice Christians who may be your friends, family members, and even your spouse. Accordingly, what follows is a pro abundant life apologetic that I believe God laid on my heart, specifically for Christians, based on Christ's own words and life. The apologetic, or argument, is organized into four questions and responses:

1. How does support for abortion fulfill the Great Commandment and the Great Commission?

2. When did Jesus's human life begin and how should this fact affect a Christian's view of abortion?

3. What does Mary's unplanned pregnancy tell Christians about the abortion decision?

4. How should uncertainty about when life begins lead a Christian to view the abortion decision?

1. How Does support for Abortion Fulfill the Great Commandment and the Great Commission?

As Christians, we are called to live out two great initiatives in our private lives: the Great Commandment and the Great Commission. These two bookends of the Christian faith represent Christ's call to all of us, and we are charged to promote and proclaim them in the public square.

The Great Commandment is found in the Gospel accounts of Matthew and Mark. Jesus also presents the Great Commandment as the answer to a question that was asked of Him in Luke 10:25–37. A lawyer comes to Him and says, "What must I do to inherit the kingdom of God?" It's a question any Christian should be asking. Of course, Jesus didn't chastise him. Instead, we read that He leaned into the question because He thought it was a good one. And He responded, "What do the scriptures say?" The lawyer responded, "You should love your God with all your heart, with all your strength, with all your soul, and with all your mind, and love your neighbor as yourself." Jesus gives him the thumbs up—this is the Great Commandment. In other parts of Scripture, Jesus teaches how all of Scripture is hanging on these truths.

One can even see the Great Commandment in the creation story in Genesis. God created Adam and then He created Adam's neighbor, Eve, from Adam's rib bone. Eve was bone of Adam's bone; so, when Adam loved Eve, he was loving her like himself, because she was, in a real sense, himself. Therefore, until sin broke this love relationship with God and between neighbors in the garden, we had the Great Commandment in action. Whenever there is conflict in any human relationship—family or society—it reflects a breakdown or violation of the Great Commandment.

Three Loves

The Great Commandment rests on three loves: love of God, love of neighbor, and love of self. When I started to reflect on this in the context of the life issue and abortion, I believe God gave me an amazing insight about the word "neighbor." In the Greek, it means "near one" or "near fellow." So, loving your neighbor as yourself means "loving your near one as you love yourself."

And when you look at the word "love" that is used in this verse, it is the highest love possible. In the Greek it is *agapē*, or agape love in English. It is a sacrificial love. The same word for love that is used in John 3:16: "For God so loved the world, that he gave his only begotten Son, that whosoever believes in him will not perish but have eternal life." It is also used in John 15:13: "Greater love has no one than this, that he lays down his life for his friends." So, per the Great Commandment, we are supposed to have a sacrificial love for our neighbors, our near ones.

How does this relate to the life issue? If a woman is pregnant, who is her nearest near one? Nearness can be considered in two ways—physical proximity and relationship proximity. Think "next of kin." In the case of a pregnant woman, it is her baby, growing in her womb. Her baby is as physically and relationally close to her as possible.

Now, if a man got a woman pregnant, who is his near one? In this context, the vulnerable woman certainly is his neighbor, but also the baby in her womb—bone of his bone and flesh of his flesh. That is his nearest near one—his next of kin.

So, whether we profess to be pro-life or pro-choice, we must as Christians ask ourselves a question: "How is the decision to abort a baby, one of God's image bearers, an act of sacrificial love toward God?" Or, more succinctly, how does aborting a child align with the Great Commandment? Remember, Jesus said this commandment is the first and greatest: to love God and to love your neighbor as yourself.

As Christians, we must then ask ourselves a second question: "How is aborting your near one, this baby in the womb, an act of sacrificial love for your neighbor?" Again, there are three inseparable loves in this passage—love for God, love for neighbor, and love for self. If you separate these loves, the virtue of the Great Commandment can become a vice. For example, if one loves God but does not love his neighbor, 1 John 4:21 declares, "And this commandment we have from him: whoever loves God must also love his brother." And, if one loves his neighbor but does not love God, that is humanism, where one's love for neighbor is not anchored in anything immutable. It is like a boat tied to another boat, but not to a dock. Things are fine until the storms and challenges of life come and your neighbor's boat starts pulling you into rough water. In those cases, we tend to cut the rope, don't we? With humanism, our neighbors can easily become lives worth sacrificing.

Indeed, abortion is an act that declares from its core, "I don't love God and I don't love my neighbor, but I do love myself." This type of self-love becomes the vice of idolatry. So the sacrificial love for others that Jesus calls us to in the Great Commandment becomes a sacrificing love for self—the vulnerable little one in the womb becomes a child sacrifice. A life worth sacrificing, not a life worth sacrificing for. The virtue becomes a vice.

The Story of the Good Samaritan

Returning to Luke, where Jesus lays out the Great Commandment, the lawyer responds to Jesus by asking, "So who is my neighbor?" The lawyer, realizing he is called to a sacrificial love, tries to narrow the scope. It's much like when Peter asked Jesus, "How many times must I forgive my brother and sister who sins against me?" Sometimes as Christians, we are tempted to minimize a higher calling when we are face to face with it. We ask questions like, "How little do I need to do to get into heaven?" But Jesus didn't answer the lawyer's question directly. He answered the question with a story: that of the Good Samaritan.

In that story, a vulnerable person—at risk and unable to advocate for himself—had been injured by robbers and left on the side of the road to die. A priest comes by but moves to the other side of the road to distance himself and get by. Later, a Levite does the same. But when a Samaritan comes along, he draws close to the dying man, binds his wounds, and takes him to an inn. He cares for the vulnerable person with a sacrifice of time, talent, and treasure.

The "people of the Book," the priest and the Levite, moved far from the near one—the neighbor. They "aborted" him in his time of vulnerability. They had their reasons—spiritual, ministry-related, political, and maybe even social justice reasons. But their reasons did not align with biblical justice, which requires sacrificial care for the vulnerable. The Samaritan's act shows us that the pursuit of righteousness (which should have been the focus of the priest and the Levite) must be linked to the pursuit of justice and mercy if we are to truly live out the agape love required by the Great Commandment.

After Jesus tells the story, He then asks the lawyer, "Now, who was a neighbor to the person who fell?" The lawyer replies, "The one who showed him mercy." Then Jesus instructs, "Go and do likewise." In other words, be a neighbor to your neighbor. The Hebrew root of the word "mercy" further bolsters the beauty of this story. The Hebrew root for the words "mercy" and "compassion" is the same root as the word for "womb." So, the Good Samaritan put this vulnerable person in a "womb." We are called to model his example by showing sacrificial love to our neighbors.

The Mercy of the Womb

The womb of a mother is a place of mercy. Indeed, our mother's womb is a point of vulnerability that we share with every other person alive today, or who has ever lived. And the only language that babies in the womb have to express themselves is their heartbeats. I believe that every baby's heartbeat says, "Have mercy…Have mercy…Have mercy." And every time a mother hears that heartbeat, she hears, "Have mercy…Have mercy…Have mercy."

For all of us living today, our mothers responded, like the Good Samaritan, with agape love. A sacrificial love that says our lives were not worth sacrificing, but rather lives worth sacrificing for. In other words, the only reason any of us are here today is because our mothers, at least in that moment, followed the Great Commandment.

That is why, when you look at the life issue through the lens of the Great Commandment, you see a uniquely Christian, pro abundant life apologetic straight from the mouth of Jesus. So, for Christians who profess to be pro-choice, they must reconcile their perspective with the Greatest Commandment of Jesus himself. Whether it's human trafficking, food security, helping the incarcerated, or caring for the poor, the Great Commandment is the standard we must use to direct our actions for every issue. When

Christians who profess to be pro-choice look at the life issue through this lens and link it to the story of the Good Samaritan, they are far more likely to come to a pro-life perspective.

The Great Commission

The other bookend of our call as Christians is the Great Commission, which is found in Matthew 28:19–20. The Great Commission calls us to make disciples and to teach them to obey all that Christ taught us.

First, what is "all that Christ taught us?" Thankfully, Christ made this simple for us when He said of the Great Commandment, "On these two commandments the whole law and the prophets depend." In other words, living out the Great Commandment prepares us to fulfill the Great Commission.

Second, we are called to make disciples…of whom? Our neighbors…our near ones. Every parent's first "discipleship calling" is to the children with whom God blesses them. For Christians professing to be pro-choice, how is aborting their children—those who they are to make disciples of Jesus Christ—an act of disciple making? That is the equivalent of missionaries going to a foreign land to make disciples and then killing everyone there; sacrificing them so that they can have better lives for themselves. In fact, this is a common criticism of some early missionary efforts; their "disciple making" consisted of subjugating and even killing those who they were called to love sacrificially.

Again, the act of abortion is a violation of the Great Commandment, but it is also a violation of the Great Commission, a calling of all followers of Christ.

2. When Did Jesus's Human Life Begin?

A Christian who professes to be pro-choice might respond to the above argument—that abortion violates the Great Commandment and the Great Commission—by saying, "I agree that Christians are supposed to have compassion and mercy on the baby in the womb. But what if I don't believe it's a baby? What if I don't believe it's a person yet?"

Accordingly, it is critical to inspect what Scripture says about "personhood." Does the Bible have a perspective on when the "contents" of an expecting mother's womb become a baby?

Many parts of Scripture address this, but looking at the life of Jesus Himself—and His experience of being like us—can make for a more compelling case for us as Christians than isolated verses.

The central question for the pro-choice Christian is, "When did Jesus's human life begin?" The answer is critical because our entire Christian faith and salvation depend upon it. Jesus was a perfect substitute for us. Was Jesus in fact both fully God and fully human? Jesus's humanity has to match our humanity in every respect or else he's not a perfect substitute for us and we are lost.

Several passages in Scripture address this principle. Hebrews 2:17 says, "Therefore he had to be made like his brothers in every respect, so that he might become a merciful and faithful high priest in the service of God, to make propitiation for the sins of the people." 1 Peter 2:24 says, "He himself [Jesus] bore our sins in his body on the tree." Colossians 2:9–10 says, "For in him the whole fullness of deity dwells bodily, and you have been filled in him, who is the head of all rule and authority."

So, if Scripture establishes Jesus as fully God and fully man, then the question becomes, "When did Jesus's humanity begin?" Isaiah 7:14 says, "Behold, the virgin shall conceive and bear a son." Here, the Bible addressed both conception and birth. Even though the mechanics of Jesus's conception were different, the reality of His conception and birth were the same as ours— "made like his brothers in every respect" (Hebrews 2:17). A helpful analogy is artificial insemination; for a child who comes into the world via artificial insemination, the initial mechanics are different from the way children typically come into the world, but the practical reality of their conception and birth are the same. From conception on, there is no difference.

This is exactly what you see in the birth of Christ, and that is why it is critically important to establish biblically that Jesus's life began at conception. Because if Jesus's human life began at conception, then ours had to begin at conception as well. If not, then Jesus cannot be the perfect substitute for us and take on our sin, and our entire faith crumbles.

So, if a Christian who professes to be pro-choice argues that you're not actually a person in the earliest stages of pregnancy—you're not actually a life—then Jesus was not a life at this stage in His humanity either. If one were to believe this, then they must also believe there was a point at which Jesus in His incarnation, God Himself, was not alive. This idea, of course, is inconsistent with the very definition of God, who can never not "be." "I Am that I Am," means that God always is. He has always been that way, and He will always be that way.

I heard a pro-choice Christian once argue that the baby in the womb is not a life but is a "potential life." I understand why a person would try to make that argument. When trying to support an abortion decision, this reasoning sounds better than, "It's a life, but a life worth sacrificing." The problem with the concept of "potential life" is that anything that has potential can be something else. A coach can say of a football player who joins his team, "That guy's got a lot of potential," but the player can turn out to be a bust. Potential is not always reality. If it is potentially something, then it potentially can be something else. But Jesus could not be a potential life in the womb. Why? Because He cannot and could not be anything else other than what He is—fully God and fully man, alive in Mary's womb from the moment of conception.

Potential also brings with it the concept of uncertainty. When you say of the football player, "He's got potential," uncertainty is built into that statement. But being God means there is no uncertainty on any matter or in any circumstance. God always operates in certainty.

This line of thinking—that there is a period of time after conception that an unborn baby is not yet a life—can lead to another dangerous fallacy: the belief that life is "constructed" in the womb. Babies are not constructed in the womb like a Tesla on an assembly line. When is a Tesla truly a Tesla? When the wheels are put on? When they put on the nameplate? I submit that a Tesla is never intrinsically a Tesla. Why? Because at any point you can turn a Tesla into a toaster. It always has the potential to be something else.

But babies are not constructed; they develop. That's why there are classes on human development, not human construction. Once conceived, a baby cannot be anything else. Much like a Polaroid picture, once you take it, it can only be what the lens saw. When you first look at an undeveloped Polaroid, it looks like a black square. But "in the fullness of time," it develops into what the lens captured, and only that. You can't take a picture of an apple and have it develop into a picture of an orange. It is intrinsically what it is and can't be anything else—just like Christ in Mary's womb and just like any baby in a mother's womb. There is no uncertainty, from the moment of conception.

3. Mary's Pregnancy with Christ

The third argument revolves around the stories we read in Luke's Gospel account of Christ's birth, Mary's pregnancy with Christ, and her visit to Elizabeth. When the angel comes to Mary and tells her that she's going to conceive and bear a child, the angel also reveals that her cousin, Elizabeth, is also going to have a child who has already been conceived.

A few aspects of this story are significant to the life issue. First, Mary faced an "unplanned pregnancy" from a human perspective. She had hopes and dreams for her life and her life with Joseph. Those hopes did not include a child at this time and in this way. Accordingly, Mary's response to this unplanned pregnancy is instructive; she chose life.

But there's more, because the angel gave Mary another piece of information that was probably not known by anybody else: her cousin, Elizabeth—known to be a barren woman past childbearing years—was pregnant with a son as well. And Scripture says that, once Elizabeth conceived, she hid herself for five months. It is unlikely anyone knew that Elizabeth was pregnant, other than her husband who could not speak. The passage ends with, "nothing is impossible for God." In the very next chapter, we are told that Mary "rose up in haste" to see Elizabeth. Why would she hurry to go see her cousin? When a woman faces an unplanned pregnancy, who does she tell first? Likely somebody who can or should sympathize with her situation. Mary's miraculous unplanned pregnancy compelled her to go see Elizabeth, who was experiencing a rather miraculous pregnancy, too. Scripture tells us that Elizabeth was about six months pregnant when Mary approached her, and when Elizabeth heard the greeting from Mary, the child jumped within her. What prompted the child inside Elizabeth's womb to jump? Jesus, of course, conceived in Mary's womb. Importantly, this was probably only days or a few weeks after Christ's conception. Remember, Mary went *in haste* to see Elizabeth.

This is significant to the life issue because Scripture tells us that both late-term abortion and early-term abortion end a human life. John the Baptist, who was in Elizabeth's womb, leaped in response to something happening outside the womb. And he was responding to a "someone," a life growing in Mary's womb.

If a Christian is uncertain about the life issue, start with the question, "When did Jesus's life begin?" Scripture makes clear when it began, but the story of Mary's visit to Elizabeth adds another finer point, affirming the presence of life in the womb in both the earliest and latest stages of pregnancy.

Importantly, none of these Scriptures mention the word "abortion," but it's clear that the principles speak to it directly.

4. How Should Uncertainty About When Life Begins Lead a Christian to View the Abortion Decision?

Despite the power of the above biblical arguments, I have encountered pro-choice Christians who generally agree with the arguments but retain their pro-choice position. Why? They are uncertain about when life begins. But is support for abortion a logical conclusion to draw from such uncertainty? As Christians, we can respond to this reasoning by asking, "Do you have a worldview that says that human life is precious?" As Christians, pro-life or pro-choice, we certainly have a worldview that says human life is precious. We can go a step further by asking, "Do you believe that innocent, vulnerable life is precious?" Universally, Christians all over the world should say, "Absolutely, yes." So, if one believes that life is precious, and that innocent, vulnerable life is especially precious, then the uncertainty of when life begins actually should lead to a pro-life position.

To drive this point, I often share an illustration: let's say I ask you to come to my house to help me move my belongings to a new home. When you arrive, there's a room full of boxes that need to be loaded onto the moving truck. Just as you are about to pick up your first box, I gasp, stop you, and say, "Oh my gosh, I messed up! There is a precious, priceless Fabergé egg in one of the boxes…but I forgot to label the box." In other words, I am uncertain about which box contains the precious item. So, as I hand you your first box, how would you treat that box? Indeed, how would you treat every box? Very carefully, I'd hope! But why? Because you do not know which box contains the precious egg, you would proceed with caution, treating every box carefully as if something precious and worth protecting could be inside. Likewise, if you don't know when life begins and you believe that life is precious, especially vulnerable life, and you don't know whether the contents of a woman's womb is a life or not, then you should be pro-life, not pro-choice. You should, logically, take the more cautious approach that protects what could be precious and valuable, not the approach that could destroy it.

Conclusion

As pro-life Christians, knowing why we are pro-life is especially important when it comes to speaking with love and truth to our pro-choice brothers and sisters in Christ. These four biblical arguments present a compelling, Scripture-based case that establish the pro-life position as central to our Christian faith.

All Christians should think about the life issue primarily through the lens of the Great Commandment and the Great Commission. How does a decision to have an abortion, assist someone in an abortion, or promote abortion in the public square line up with the Great Commandment and the Great Commission?

Next, all Christians should wrestle with the question of when Jesus's human life began. Scripture is clear that His life began at conception. We can also put a finer point on this perspective by studying Mary and Elizabeth's pregnancies, which show life at the earliest and latest stages of pregnancy.

Finally, if a Christian is still uncertain about when life begins, but believes that life is precious, then their uncertainty should lead to a pro-life perspective.

YVETTE'S OPEN LETTER

To College-Bound Women Who Might Face an Unplanned Pregnancy

Back in 2021, Texas teen Paxton Smith gave a passionate – and unapproved – valedictorian speech at her high school graduation ceremony expressing her personal opinions and concerns about pro-life state laws and the "war" they pose on her body and her rights. My wife, Yvette, being a "Texas girl" herself who faced an unplanned pregnancy in her sophomore year of college, wrote an open letter to the young women in Ms. Smith's graduating class. This letter is relevant to any young woman who is college-bound and may one day face an unplanned pregnancy of her own; I pray it makes an impact on them, too.

Dear Graduates,

I'm a Texas girl. I was born and raised in San Antonio. I graduated from Thomas Edison High School. When I heard Paxton Smith's valedictorian address at your recent graduation ceremony, I was taken back to my days as a hopeful 18-year-old, ready to go out into the world to achieve my hopes and dreams.

But can you guess what happened just two years after I graduated from high school? I got pregnant. I was a sophomore at Princeton University.

The reason I need you to hear my story is because what Ms. Paxton told you is not the whole story.

Can you imagine how I felt when I found out I was pregnant? Fourth overall in my high school class, top girl in the class, yearbook editor, club president, first person in my family to attend a prestigious Ivy League university…

So, when I visited the health center at Princeton, the nurse told me exactly what Ms. Paxton told you at your graduation. She told me my hopes and dreams of graduating and becoming a doctor would be dead, would not happen, if I had a baby. "Of course" I should have an abortion, she said. After all, it was my right.

Dear young women, by God's grace, I did not do what the nurse told me to do. I graduated from Princeton. I attended Temple University Medical School, one of the top programs in the nation, and became the Chief Resident in my family practice residency. I was then a distinguished graduate in officer training school in the Air Force, where I spent the next four years. I was a Major when I left the Air Force and was honored as the medical "provider of the year" during my tenure.

I have been practicing medicine for about 30 years. I have lots of certificates and degrees hanging on my wall. But the accomplishment I value and cherish the most is bringing my son into the world. The baby who I was told to "throw away" graduated from Harvard University and is a blessing to me and so many others. You see, my degrees and awards will fade, but the joy from my decision to have my son is eternal. He was not a life worth sacrificing. He was a life worth sacrificing for.

So, unlike Ms. Paxton, I have seen what your future can be because I lived it. Do not believe the deception that you have to dehumanize another in order to preserve your own humanity. Do not believe that the only way you will "matter" is if you exercise your rights at the expense of your baby's right to life.

I have been you, but you haven't been me…yet. By God's grace, you will achieve your hopes and dreams, like I did, without regretting the choices you make along the way.

I believe in you. Fear not, because you are strong and can handle whatever life throws at you. Now go out there and love others, serve others, and do all the great things you aspire to do!

Praying for the best for you,
Yvette Lopez-Warren, M.D.

Use the QR code below to share Yvette's letter to a college-bound women who might be facing an unplanned pregnancy:

ABOUT CARE NET

Founded in 1975, Care Net is a pro abundant life ministry whose vision is a culture where women and men faced with pregnancy decisions are transformed by the gospel of Jesus Christ and empowered to choose life for their unborn children and abundant life for their families. Acknowledging that every human life begins at conception and is worthy of protection, Care Net offers compassion, hope, and help to anyone considering abortion by presenting them with realistic alternatives and Christ-centered support through our life-affirming network of pregnancy centers, churches, organizations, and individuals.

Support Care Net

At a time when millions of women and men are searching for answers to their unplanned, unexpected, or unexpectedly complicated pregnancies, we must act now to help them choose life for their unborn children and abundant life for their families. By donating to Care Net, you will ensure that:

- there's always a coach ready to take a call on Care Net's national hotline from a parent considering abortion,
- our 1,200 affiliated pregnancy centers are equipped to serve their communities to save babies from abortion and build strong families,
- churches will become places of hope and healing for those facing unplanned pregnancies and those seeking healing from past abortions, and pro-life people can access free resources to learn how to turn their pro-life passion into pro abundant life action.

Since 2008, generous pro-life people have saved more than 1 million babies from abortion and shared the gospel with more than two million parents. Your donation to Care Net will ensure that women and men find the life-affirming resources they need to choose life for their unborn children and abundant life for their families. Donate today at https://donate. care-net.org/carenet/save-lives or use the QR code.

NOTES

CHAPTER TWO

1. Gary W. Moon, *Homesick for Eden* (Ann Arbor, MI: Vine Books, 1997).

2. Katherine Kortsmit, Antoinette T. Nguyen, et al., "Abortion Surveillance—United States, 2020," Centers for Disease Control, Morbidity and Mortality Weekly Report, *Surveillance Summaries*, 2022;71(No. SS-10):1–27. DOI: https://www.cdc.gov/mmwr/volumes/71/ss/ss7110a1.htm#T7_down.

CHAPTER THREE

1. Katherine Kortsmit, Antoinette T. Nguyen, et al., "Abortion Surveillance—United States, 2020," Centers for Disease Control, Morbidity and Mortality Weekly Report, *Surveillance Summaries*, 2022;71(No. SS-10):1–27. DOI: https://www.cdc.gov/mmwr/volumes/71/ss/ss7110a1.htm#T7_down.

2. Carl R. Trueman, *Strange New World: How Thinkers and Activists Redefined Identity and Sparked the Sexual Revolution* (Wheaton, IL: Crossway, 2022), 66.

3. Ibid., 66.

4. Mary Elizabeth Williams, "So what if abortion ends a life?" *Salon*, January, 23, 2013, https://www.salon.com/2013/01/23/so_what_if_abortion_ends_life/.

5. Ibid.

6. Cody Derespina, "'Comedians in Cars Getting Abortions' video outrages both sides of debate," Fox News Online, July 14, 2016, https://www.foxnews.com/us/comedians-in-cars-getting-abortions-video-outrages-both-sides-of-debate.

7. Bradford Richardson, "Hillary Clinton: 'Unborn Person' Has No Constitutional Rights." *Washington Times*, April 3, 2016, https://www.washingtontimes.com/news/2016/apr/3/hillary-clinton-unborn-person-has-no-constitutiona/.

8. Jessica Tarlov, "Pregnancy Made Me More Pro-Choice," *Romper*, February 20, 2024, https://www.romper.com/pregnancy/pregnancy-made-me-more-pro-choice.

9. Isaac Maddow-Zimmet and Candace Gibson, "Despite Bans, Number of Abortions in the United States Increased in 2023," Guttmacher Institute, March 19, 2024, https://www.guttmacher.org/2024/03/despite-bans-number-abortions-united-states-increased-2023.

10. Susan Milligan, "U.S. Abortions Increase in Year After Supreme Court Decision," *U.S. News & World Report*, October 24, 2023, https://www.us-news.com/news/national-news/articles/2023-10-24/u-s-abortions-increase-in-year-after-supreme-court-decision.

11. Katherine Kortsmit, PhD, Antoinette T. Nguyen, et al., "Abortion Surveillance," Centers for Disease Control and Prevention Morbidity and Mortality Weekly Report, November 24, 2023, http://dx.doi.org/10.15585/mmwr.ss7209a1.

12. Dawn Stacey, "Why Do People Have Abortions?" Verywellhealth.com, August 7, 2023, https://www.verywellhealth.com/reasons-for-abortion-906589#citation-6.

CHAPTER FOUR

1. George A. Akerlof and Janet L. Yellen, "An analysis of out-of-wedlock births in the United States," Brookings Institution.edu, August 1, 1996, https://www.brookings.edu/articles/an-analysis-of-out-of-wedlock-births-in-the-united-states/.

2. U.S. Census Bureau, Current Population Survey, America's Families and Living Arrangements: Table C-8: "Poverty Status, Food Stamp Receipt, and Public Assistance for Children Under 18 Years," November 2021, https://www2.census.gov/programs-surveys/demo/tables/families/2021/cps-2021/.

3. Care Net and Lifeway Research, "Care Net Study of American Men Whose Partner Has Had an Abortion: A Survey of 1,000 American Men," 2021, https://research.lifeway.com/wp-content/uploads/2022/01/Care-Net-2021-Report.pdf.

4. Ibid.

5. Ibid.

CHAPTER FIVE

1. U.S. Census Bureau, America's Families and Living Arrangements: Table C-3: "Living Arrangements of Children Under 18 Years and Marital Status of Parents by Age, Sex, Race, and Hispanic Origin and Selected Characteristics of the Child for all Children," 2018, https://www.census.gov/data/tables/2018/demo/families/cps-2018.html.

2. National Fatherhood Initiative, "Father Facts, 8th Edition: Consequences of Father Absence for Children," 2019, p. 11.

3. Susan Yoon, Fei Pei, et al., "Vulnerability or resilience to early substance use among adolescents at risk: The roles of maltreatment and father involvement," *Child Abuse and Neglect*, 2018; 86, 206-216.

4. J. Mandara, S. Y. Rogers, & R. E. Zinbarg, "The effects of family structure on African American adolescents' marijuana use," *Journal of Marriage and Family*, 2011; 73(3), 557–569.

5. Sage Kim and Elizabeth Glassgow, "The effect of father's absence, parental adverse events, and neighborhood disadvantage on children's aggression and delinquency: A multi-analytic approach," *Journal of Human Behavior in the Social Environment*, 2018; 28, 570-587.

6. Elena Mariani, Berkay Ozcan, and Alice Goisis, "Family trajectories and well-being of children born to lone mothers in the UK," *European Journal of Population*, March 23, 2017; 33, 185-215.

7. Amina Alio, Alfred Mbah, et al., "Assessing the Impact of Paternal Involvement on Racial/Ethnic Disparities in Infant Mortality Rates," *Journal of Community Health*, 2011; 36(1), 63-68.

8. S. Zhang and T. Fuller, "Neighborhood disorder and paternal involvement of nonresident and resident fathers," *Family Relations*, 2012; 61(3), 501-513.

9. Ibid.

10. Catherine Salmon, John Townsend, and Jessica Hehman, "Casual Sex and College Students: Sex Differences and the Impact of Father Absence," *Evolutionary Psychological Science*, July 1, 2016; 2, 254-261.

11. Samuel W. Sturgeon, "The Relationship Between Family Structure and Adolescent Sexual Activity," The Heritage Foundation, November 14, 2008.

12. Bruce J. Ellis, John E. Bates, et al., "Does father absence place daughters at special risk for early sexual activity and teenage pregnancy?" *Child Development*, May 16, 2003; 74, 801-821.

CHAPTER SIX

1. Samuel W. Sturgeon, "The Relationship Between Family Structure and Adolescent Sexual Activity," The Heritage Foundation, November 14, 2008.

2. Katherine Kortsmit, Antoinette T. Nguyen, et al., "Abortion Surveillance—United States, 2020," Centers for Disease Control, Morbidity and Mortality Weekly Report, *Surveillance Summaries*, 2022;71(No. SS-10):1–27. DOI: http://dx.doi.org/10.15585/mmwr.ss7110a1.

3. U.S. Census Bureau, Historical Marital Status Tables, November 2023, https://www.census.gov/data/tables/time-series/demo/families/marital.html.

4. Lydia Anderson, Chanell Washington, et al., "Home Alone: More Than a Quarter of All Households Have One Person," U.S. Census Bureau, June 8, 2023, https://www.census.gov/library/stories/2023/06/more-than-a-quarter-all-households-have-one-person.html

CHAPTER SEVEN

1. Care Net and Lifeway Research, "Study of Women Who Have Had an Abortion and Their Views on the Church," 2015, https://research.lifeway.com/wp-content/uploads/2015/11/Care-Net-Final-Presentation-Report-Revised.pdf.

2. Care Net and Lifeway Research, "Care Net Study of American Men Whose Partner Has Had an Abortion: A Survey of 1,000 American Men," 2021, https://care-net.org/mens-survey/.

3. Rachel K. Jones, "People of All Religions Use Birth Control and Have Abortions," Guttmacher Institute, October 2020, https://www.guttmacher.org/article/2020/10/people-all-religions-use-birth-control-and-have-abortions.

4. Care Net and Lifeway Research, "Study of Women Who Have Had an Abortion and Their Views on the Church," 2015, https://research.lifeway.com/wp-content/uploads/2015/11/Care-Net-Final-Presentation-Report-Revised.pdf.

CHAPTER EIGHT

1. Susan Cohen, "Repeat Abortion, Repeat Unintended Pregnancy, Repeated and Misguided Government Policies," Guttmacher Policy Review, Volume 10: Issue 2, May 17, 2007, https://www.guttmacher.org/gpr/2007/05/repeat-abortion-repeat-unintended-pregnancy-repeated-and-misguided-government-policies.

CHAPTER NINE

1. Aaron Earls, "Some Churches Partner with Pregnancy Centers After *Roe v. Wade* Reversal," Lifeway Research Summary, June 18,2024, https://research.lifeway.com/2024/06/18/some-churches-partner-with-pregnancy-centers-after-roe-v-wade/.

FRAMEWORK ONE

1. U.S. Supreme Court, *Dobbs v. Jackson Women's Health Organization*, June 24, 2022, https://www.courtlistener.com/opinion/6481357/dobbs-v-jackson-womens-health-organization/.
2. Josh Hicks, "Romney's Official Stance on Abortion," *The Washington Post*, October 22, 2012, https://www.washingtonpost.com/blogs/fact-checker/post/romneys-official-stance-on-abortion/2012/10/20/f7bd00dc-1a3d-11e2-aa6f-3b636fecb829_blog.html.
3. National Park Service, "Lincoln on Slavery," Last updated April 10, 2015, https://www.nps.gov/liho/learn/historyculture/slavery.htm.
4. Abraham Lincoln, "Lincoln's First Inaugural Address," Published on American Battlefield Trust, https://www.battlefields.org/learn/primary-sources/lincolns-first-inaugural-address?ms=googlepaid&gad_source=1&gclid=CjwKCAjwo6GyBhBwEiwAzQTmc9t-Xp5xdAhQ4PsHc5ZJ6qF3KFU2UkuxJR-b9npYi-jwuRMeQj-u4RoCifsQAvD_BwE.
5. Abraham Lincoln, "Lincoln's Second Inaugural Address," Lincoln Memorial page, National Park Service, Updated April 18, 2020, https://www.nps.gov/linc/learn/historyculture/lincoln-second-inaugural.htm.

6. Frederick Douglass National Historic Site of District of Columbia, "Confronting a President: Douglass and Lincoln," National Parks Service, Updated July 24, 2021, https://www.nps.gov/frdo/learn/historyculture/confronting-a-president-douglass-and-lincoln.htm.

7. Richard John Neuhaus, *The Naked Public Square: Religion and Democracy in America*, (Grand Rapids: W.B. Eerdmans, 1984), 132.

8. Ohio Issue 1, Right to Make Reproductive Decisions Including Abortion Initiative, Ballotpedia.org, 2023, https://ballotpedia.org/Ohio_Issue_1,_Right_to_Make_Reproductive_Decisions_Including_Abortion_Initiative_(2023).

9. Rachel K. Jones, "People of All Religions Use Birth Control and Have Abortions," Guttmacher Institute, October 2020, https://www.guttmacher.org/article/2020/10/people-all-religions-use-birth-control-and-have-abortions.

FRAMEWORK THREE

1. Mary Elizabeth Williams, "So what if abortion ends a life?" *Salon*, January, 23, 2013, https://www.salon.com/2013/01/23/so_what_if_abortion_ends_life/.

FRAMEWORK FOUR

1. Lawrence B. Finer, Lori F. Frohwirth, et al., "Reasons U.S. Women Have Abortions: Quantitative and Qualitative Perspectives," *Perspectives on Sexual and Reproductive Health* Volume 37, Number 3, September 2005, https://www.guttmacher.org/sites/default/files/article_files/3711005.pdf.

FRAMEWORK FIVE

1. Men4Choice, "About Us," Accessed July 18, 2024, https://www.men4choice.org/about/

2. Unite for Gender and Reproductive & Gender Equity (URGE), Accessed March 17, 2018, https://urge.org/bro-choice-links-2/

3. Scott Calvert, "These Men Are on The Front Lines of the Abortion-Rights Movement," *The Wall Street Journal*, June 30, 2024, https://www.wsj.com/us-news/young-men-abortion-rights-movement-19c643ec?mod=e2tw

Made in the USA
Las Vegas, NV
16 October 2024

c2c12d7a-3f5e-478e-b404-27181f7d1d82R02